BRAIN FITNESS

BRAIN FITNESS

—

Monique Le Poncin

Doctor of Science

WITH MICHEL LEVINE
TRANSLATED BY LOWELL BAIR

FAWCETT COLUMBINE · NEW YORK

To my son Christophe
and to my parents.

A Fawcett Columbine Book
Published by Ballantine Books

Translation copyright © 1990 by Random House, Inc.

Library of Congress Catalog Card Number: 89-92590

ISBN: 0-449-90348-6

Text design by Holly Johnson

Manufactured in the United States of America

First American Edition: November 1990
10 9 8 7 6 5 4 3 2

CONTENTS

IMPORTANT NOTE TO THE READER

The purpose of this book is to increase the reader's awareness of his or her brain. The exercises proposed in it are therefore difficult to do with complete success, within their allotted times.

It is important not to use this book as a basis for collective courses; there are appropriate training programs that should be requested from the INRPVC.*

---

* Institut National de Recherche sur la Prévention du Vieillissement Cérébral (National Institute for Research on the Prevention of Cerebral Aging), Hôpital Bicêtre, 78, rue du Général-Leclerc, 94275 Le Kremlin-Bicêtre, France.

BRAIN FITNESS

PREFACE AND TEST

Every day at the INRPVC, I and my team of physicians, psychologists, and biologists talk with men and women who have cerebral problems that make them live in anxiety and sometimes even in anguish.

Most of them are not "sick," and we never regard them as such at the outset. All of them, whatever their age—and their average age is steadily decreasing—feel a need to get their bearings and put an end to the questions and doubts assailing them.

What do they usually say to us in their first interview?

"I retired two years ago. At first everything was fine; then I began feeling a kind of emptiness, as if my brain were getting numb. I tried to take an interest in new things, broaden my horizon, but it didn't work. Now I don't enjoy anything and I'm afraid of turning into a kind of vegetable."

"My boss has asked me to learn a foreign language very quickly. But no matter how hard I try, I just can't get it into my head. My mind is closed and I can't open it. Time is passing; I know I won't learn the language, and then . . . "

"It's terrible; every time I go on vacation to a foreign country, I have trouble converting money, and I can't remember phone numbers, especially if I have to use an area code. . . . And I'm only fifty-five! I read somewhere that by that age a lot of brain cells have died off and the process of mental aging is already under way. But isn't there something I can do about it?"

"Ever since I lost my job I've been trying to take retraining courses, but I don't feel up to it. I really wish I could get back to where I was, but every day it seems like I'm falling farther behind everyone else. I don't know what's going to happen to me."

"It's funny—it all started when my son beat me in tennis for the first time! I put away my racket, and then I gradually started losing interest in things. I can feel myself sliding, drifting into a kind of indifference. At fifty-seven, it just doesn't make sense!"

"After my divorce I had to start earning a living again, but it's unbelievable how much I lost during those years. The work isn't done the same way anymore, and I feel rusty. No matter how hard I try, it takes me twice as long to do things as the other women. It can't go on like that, of course. Is there any way I can avoid being a failure?"

"Everyone who knows me will tell you I'm hyperactive, a real glutton for work! Six months ago I had an operation, and . . . Physically, I came out of it just fine, no problems. But something seems to have gone wrong with my mind. I forget things, I'm absentminded, I mix up names—nothing very serious, actually, and luckily my secretary is there to make up for my lapses, but I can't help worrying about whether it's going to get worse."

"There's nothing wrong with me, I'm sure of that, but I must admit I'm really upset about what's happened to my mother. She was in very good shape as far as her mind was concerned, still sharp as a tack, and then suddenly she went downhill so fast I couldn't believe it. It's terrible! And I wonder if someday it will happen to me."

Similar things could be said by many people who do not have the courage, or simply the opportunity, to talk with us as our visitors at the institute do. Those visitors have made an effort to overcome their shyness and apprehension. They have often had to face the misgivings and prejudices of their friends and relatives. "You haven't gotten to the point where you need help," they have been told. "Anyway, nothing can be done about the way someone's mind works. There's no way to change it. Going to that place will just be a waste of time."

Many men and women are reluctant to talk about their difficulties, and often do not admit them even to themselves. But their concerns are clearly reflected by questions asked during meetings of discussion groups that I conduct within organizations for older people. Many of the doctors I meet during scientific conferences tell me that increasing numbers of their patients are worried about a decline in their mental abilities: "Doctor, sometimes I can't remember things I know perfectly well, I make embarrassing mistakes by confusing one of my friends with another, I can't manage to work electronic devices that are supposed to be very simple to use. Is my mind going bad?" These doctors are often at a loss when they hear such questions; in medical school they have studied aphasia and memory disorders from a neurophysiological viewpoint, but they were not taught how to treat them. The institute now gives them information and tells them about procedures to follow.

To put the question in a more general way, which of us, at one time or another in our social or professional lives, has never had the feeling of being unable to keep pace with our constantly changing world?

Those who miss chances for self-improvement and success will quickly find themselves in the situation of a man who has fallen overboard in a stormy sea: if he is not a skilled swimmer in good condition, he will not be able to reach any of the few life preservers thrown to him and will soon sink.

In our world of relentless competition, people who have met with a failure are often shoved aside, which worsens their problems. Because of their self-doubt and anxiety, and their feeling that they are victims of injustice, that others have "left them in the lurch," they withdraw into themselves and give up. In doing so, they cut themselves off from everything that might stimulate their minds and help them to compete effectively, and they gradually sink into a kind of irremediable mental lethargy. It should be added that certain medicines, especially tranquilizers, whose use is steadily growing, may contribute to that psychic deterioration.

Society is condemning people more and more quickly, and at an increasingly early age, for not being perfectly adapted to its pace. The most rational and effective way to help those "misfits" is not—as is still done, unfortunately—to confine them in the various ghettos of social exclusion, but to help them stay aboard the ship among the other members of the crew, while teaching them to become good swimmers in case of trouble.

Our institute is devoted to that task. We use a technique of cerebral activation that I have developed and named Brain Fitness.

How do we proceed? First of all, before new arrivals begin their actual "training," we convince them that they must get rid of their anxieties and preconceived ideas. No, nothing is inevitable where the brain is concerned; deterioration of the body does not inescapably bring on deterioration of the mind. No, there is not necessarily something wrong with their brain, contrary to what they may think—or to what others may try to make them think. *They are simply using only a minute part of their cerebral resources, leaving the rest in a state of quiescence.*

How does Brain Fitness work? By means of specific exercises, it revives mental abilities that may have fallen into dormancy, or are working only in slow motion, and brings them back to full efficiency. Then, with the return of self-confidence, a new impetus is given to the vital force that we all have within us, the little flame that still burns, flickering, even when we think all is lost.

We soon see men and women who had thought they were condemned to failure and isolation lose their gnawing sense of inferiority and achieve cerebral autonomy, that is, the ability to take responsibility for themselves and feel involved in the running of the world. We have restored their independence and freedom. They are no longer a burden to their families or society.

I want to make it clear that our team does not claim to work miracles, to turn out Einsteins and Inaudis. We simply develop the previously unknown fertility of land that had been lying fallow.

The activities of the institute are not, of course, limited to that

work. It plays a leading part in applied neurophysiological research, trains a certain number of physicians and biologists, and,
above all, strives to make the public increasingly aware of the
crucially important idea that diminished mental efficiency must no
longer be regarded as inevitable, but can be fought and overcome.

I will now offer you a little exercise that will help you to enter
into the spirit of Brain Fitness. It is by no means a scientific test.
It is intended only to give an indication of your cerebral efficiency.

Take a pencil, read the forty statements and mark the ones
that seem to apply to you. Be as honest as possible, because otherwise the exercise will be of no value. Keep a record of your score,
and later, when you have learned the technique of Brain Fitness,
repeat the exercise—I'm willing to bet that you'll have some happy
surprises!

1. When I want to park my car, it often takes me so long to
   decide between two vacant places that I lose my chance
   to park in either of them. ☐

2. I often forget to turn off a light, close a window, etc., when
   I leave my house or apartment. ☐

3. When I buy a new appliance, I first try to find out how it
   works by handling it; only if that fails do I read the instructions, and I often consider them badly written. ☐

4. In the supermarket, I feel lost when certain items are put
   in a different place or, even worse, when a whole department is relocated. I go to the wrong aisle several days in
   a row before I finally get used to the new arrangement. ☐

5. I often forget where I've put commonly used things: my
   keys, glasses, wallet, pen, address book, etc. ☐

6. I'm clumsy whenever I have to use my hands for such things as playing a game of skill, opening a can, or repairing something. ☐

7. It's unbelievable how quickly I get annoyed by children playing around me! I love them, but they still complicate my life. ☐

8. I often mix up the names of television personalities I know quite well. ☐

9. During the first few months of the year, it's not unusual for me to date a check with the year before. ☐

10. I often know the right answers when I watch a television game show, but I nearly always say them too late. ☐

11. I don't care much about my physical appearance; to me, elegance is something superficial that concerns only other people. ☐

12. I can't remember my Social Security number or the number of my credit card. ☐

13. I feel that life wouldn't be worth living if I had an important handicap, such as blindness, loss of a hand, or a serious disease. ☐

14. I'm distressed at the thought of going to a country where I would have to contend with a foreign language. ☐

15. I know some jokes perfectly well, but when I tell one of them I often leave out an important detail, or get part of it wrong, or mangle the punch line—in other words, I often make it fall flat. ☐

16. I'm convinced that I won't live to be very old. ☐

17. When I watch TV I often switch channels, even while a program is still going on, because I get tired of things quickly. ☐

18. To be sure I won't forget anything, I have to make out a list before I go shopping, and I feel lost if I don't remember to take it with me. ☐

19. Even if I have a detailed map of a part of town where I have to go, once I get there I can't manage to locate the streets and find the right direction, and there's nothing for me to do but ask someone for help. ☐

20. If I talk about music, clothes, or politics with my children or grandchildren, the discussion soon turns into an argument. ☐

21. Every time I get on an airplane I ask the flight attendant where my seat is instead of looking at my boarding pass. ☐

22. Fairly often I forget something on the stove or in the oven (water, eggs, meat, etc.). ☐

23. When I look at vacation photographs, I often can't remember where or when they were taken. ☐

24. If I inherited a large sum of money, I would immediately think of giving it to a child, a charity, or a humanitarian organization, rather than spending it on myself. ☐

25. When I have to calculate a percentage, I must use a pencil and a piece of paper. ☐

26. When I buy another car, it takes me a long time to get used to driving it. ☐

27. I hate it when any of my things are put in a different place! ☐

28. Sometimes I can't remember a newspaper article even though I read it only a short time ago. ☐

29. When a traffic light turns green, I often hear drivers behind me honking their horns because they feel I haven't started quickly enough. ☐

30. If my doorbell rings when I'm busy doing something that takes close attention, I feel a kind of panic and it takes me a while to make up my mind to stop working and go to the door. ☐

31. When I've already put sugar in my coffee or tea, or salt on my food, I sometimes forget and do it again. ☐

32. I stumble over new words, especially names, and once I've gotten into the habit of mispronouncing one, I have a hard time getting used to pronouncing it correctly. ☐

33. When I hear a phone number, I have to write it down immediately because I know I can't remember it, even if I'm going to call it within the next few minutes. ☐

34. If I discover that some of my money is missing, my first thought is that someone has stolen it. ☐

35. I sometimes greet people in the street, then realize that I've made a mistake when I see them look at me in surprise. ☐

36. It's hard for me to get to sleep in a bed other than my own, and it's not unusual for me to stay awake all night. ☐

37. Every time I try to take out money from an automatic teller I punch in the wrong code or I confuse the steps and have to start over. ☐

38. There are two towns—or teams, or events, etc.—that I always confuse with each other. ☐

39. Only my own professional milieu, past or present, really interests me. I don't care much about any others. ☐

40. If one of my usual stores goes out of business, I'm rather upset and it takes me a long time to decide on another one. ☐

What is your total?

Fewer than five statements marked? At present, what I have been discussing does not concern you—unless you have been a bit too optimistic. In that case, I advise you to read over the statements again and make yourself respect the truth, even if it hurts your vanity a little.

From five to thirty? In varying degrees, that amount of ineffectiveness should be regarded as a possible risk.

From thirty to forty? You probably tend to underestimate yourself, to consider something a common fault of yours even if it occurs only sporadically. Read over the statements again, this time being less strict—or less pessimistic.

But now let's forget figures. What matters most is the *state of mind* in which you interpreted your score.

Your total worried you? Don't take it too seriously: the "test" is only a game and has nothing scientific about it, as I have said. The fact that it made you aware of the problem, however, is positive: you will be motivated to attack your weaknesses and overcome them.

Perhaps you merely shrugged your shoulders and thought, "Yes, I marked quite a lot of the statements, but we all have our little quirks and peculiarities. They're part of life, and basically they're insignificant." If so, you may be one of those people who, when they have a toothache, refuse to see a dentist, say it's nothing serious and will soon go away, and eventually end up in a dentist's chair with a solid case of dental decay requiring long and painful treatment, whereas they would have had much less trouble if they had dealt with the problem when it started.

At the INRPVC we often see people who tell us that at first they had that reaction of indifference or refusal, but that, unfortunately, life made them realize the need for a radical change of attitude. Some of them, thinking they were better at their work than anyone else, were supplanted by a colleague or a newcomer considered to have more mental agility and capability, and they then saw the threat of extended unemployment hanging over them. For others, it was the death of a spouse or other loved one, or the abrupt change of life caused by retirement, that made them lose heart.

I am not saying that such a fate lies in store for you. I simply believe that by exercising your mind in the same way a first-class athlete maintains his body, Brain Fitness can "keep you in shape" so that you will be better able to overcome the obstacles in life, and can also give you the extra advantage you will need if you encounter a hurdle higher than the others.

This athletic imagery is not fortuitous: when great athletes are seriously injured, they heal more quickly than the average person. There was recently the case of a Formula One racing driver who suffered many fractures and lesions and had such a rapid recovery that it was called miraculous. But there was nothing supernatural about it: the healing process was greatly accelerated because he had always kept his muscles and his whole body in excellent condition, and because he had the attitude of a winner.

By practicing Brain Fitness you can achieve better performance and the ability to withstand and overcome adversity. You must, however, be convinced of one thing at all times: that nothing effective can be achieved unless you feel a desire to take yourself in hand, unless your will is stronger than your moods.

Have you firmly decided to make the commitment?

Good, let's begin!

A JOURNEY
INTO THE
MECHANISM
OF THE BRAIN

I am convinced that to act effectively we must know the how and why of things. Otherwise we grope our way, going around in circles and getting lost. If the will to make progress, and the motivations that underlie our effort, do not rest on a strong enough foundation, we may break down along the way.

It therefore seems to me essential for you to have at least a general idea of the functioning (and malfunctioning) of the part of yourself that will now be the object of your care and concern: your brain. Because that wonderful mechanism is highly complex, as you will see, now and then I will slip in a few little exercises to help you make your way through this introduction to it.

HOW YOUR BRAIN
WORKS

Surprising as it may seem, the human race took a very long time to recognize the real importance of the brain. The ancient Egyptians were convinced that the seat of thought and feeling was not in that gray, wrinkled, apparently inert mass, but in the diaphragm, and especially the heart, the "noble," rhythmically moving organ which distributed that vital, almost magic liquid: blood. For centuries it was regarded as the seat of the passions (and still is, symbolically and poetically). The first scientific work on the brain was not written until the Renaissance, and only in the late nineteenth century did it become possible, thanks to sophisticated methods of investigation, to make a more thorough study of that still mysterious organ. (The technique of microscopic examination of brain tissue dates from 1875, and it was in 1906 that two neurophysiologists, Camillo Golgi and Santiago Ramón y Cajal, won a Nobel Prize for their research on the structure of the nervous system.) It should be noted that, until rather recently, legal death was defined by the cessation of the heartbeat, while now it is defined by the cessation of brain functioning (a "flat" encephalogram).

We now know that the brain, extended by the spinal cord, governs the functioning of the body, including all its organs and senses. It controls a network of nerves that brings it information and transmits its orders, conveyed by various chemical substances and electric currents. All this forms what is called the nervous system.

In recent years, advanced neurophysiological techniques have greatly increased our knowledge of how this system works. At the same time—and this is typical of many scientific disciplines—researchers have discovered that what was thought to be simple is actually quite complex. As problems have been solved, new questions have often arisen. The brain system is particularly difficult to study for two main reasons: first, it works at prodigious speed, using intricate electric and chemical processes for multiple and highly diversified tasks, which pushes observation devices to the limits of their capability; and second, it is the seat of "thought," and there the scientist must proceed with caution and humility.

Now that I have said a few words about the complexity of the brain system, and the shadowy areas in our knowledge of it, I will give a highly simplified description of its functioning.

We will begin with an apparently ordinary event and use it as a reference as we make our way through that world: while you are walking along the street, you see a poster that catches your attention.

How does this take place? First, an image of the poster is formed on your retina and is analyzed there by thousands of special cells, called cones and rods, which transform it into a certain number of electric signals that constitute what is known as a nerve impulse. (This is somewhat similar to a microphone's transformation of sound waves into electric signals.) At the same time, other sense organs (those of the ears, the nose, the skin) take in other data (a sound of laughter, the smell of food frying in a nearby restaurant, a sensation of warmth) that are also transformed into electric signals. To this is added an emotional charge (passing mood, aesthetic pleasure, disapproval, etc.). Thus several senses are utilized to form a composite message.*

---

* This phenomenon is not limited to the outer environment: if you have a stomachache, for example, it is because you have been alerted by sense organs in your stomach.

Seeing and hearing are natural functional activities that we begin as soon as we are born. But if a kitten is raised in surroundings where it sees only vertical lines, it will later be incapable of distinguishing horizontal structures. From this we may conclude that we must "break in" the instruments of perception we are born with, because otherwise they will not function to the best of their ability in later life. In that "breaking in," the social factor plays an important part: others help us to train our own functions. Children with no one to talk to them will not learn to speak (as has been seen in the case of "wolf children"). At the other end of the age spectrum, old people placed in isolation will suffer more rapid deterioration of their sensory functions than if they had gone on living in a normal social environment.

Starting from the sense organs, nerve impulses reach the brain by way of nerve cells known as neurons.

Neurons are extremely numerous: each of us has about fourteen billion of them at birth. They do not reproduce, and their number diminishes through the years, as we will see. Their shapes and sizes vary with their functions, and they may be clustered together in groups. They form within the body a kind of close-meshed network that is constantly under tension.

A typical neuron (see figure 1) is the site of three main activities. First, reception of nerve impulses; this is done by the dendrites. Second, conduction of the impulses through the axon, which might be described as the "arm" of the neuron. Third, transmission to the next neuron across the synapse. Note that the two neurons do not touch each other at the synapse; the space between them is called the synapse. This is where transmission of the nerve impulse, and therefore of information, takes place, by means of chemical substances (acetylcholine, norepinephrine, dopamine, serotonin, etc.) known as neurotransmitters.

Whether it is doing this work or is simply "on the alert," ready to do it at any moment, the neuron needs energy. The cell body produces energy by consuming the glucose and oxygen brought to it by nearby blood vessels as fine as hair (hence their name— capillaries, from the Latin *capillaris*, "hair"). The function of this miniature power station is called the metabolism of the neuron.

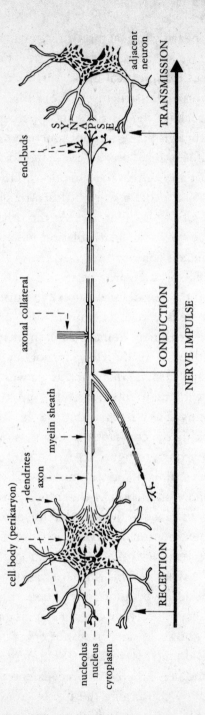

Figure 1—Diagram of a neuron

Each neuron, then, is a little world that performs its function and assures its own nutrition. We have here taken the example of neurons that conduct electric signals to the brain (sensory neurons), but others (motoneurons) transmit orders from the brain to the muscles, for example, by various pathways, such as the spinal cord.

When we make any movement or manifest the slightest reaction, a very large number of neurons must go into action. Simply standing, balanced on our legs, involves many neurons within the elaborate network that acts at every moment of our lives. The term "neuronal man" has been used with good reason.

Once it reaches the brain, a nerve impulse is taken over by other neurons, which make it follow a very complex circuit.

If we were to remove a person's brainpan, we would see a gray, furrowed mass richly supplied with blood. This mass is called the brain. Its weight is generally estimated at about three pounds, but it may vary from one individual to another. It represents about one-fortieth of the body's weight. I have bad news for those who still believe—as many believed for a long time—that this proportion is a sign of human superiority in intelligence: we are beaten by the marmoset and the ferret, whose brains account for a twelfth of their body weight.

Seventy-five percent of the brain is composed of water and various cells, mainly neurons. Some of them are distributed over the surface of the brain, in the cortex (a Latin word meaning "tree bark"), and below the surface in the form of nuclei, constituting the "gray matter." The fibers coming into and out of these neurons make up what is called the "white matter."

Three important parts can be distinguished in the brain: the cerebrum, consisting of the left and right hemispheres; the cerebellum; and, connecting them with the spinal cord, the brain stem (see figure 2). The main function of the cerebellum is coordinating our movements—in standing, walking, swimming, and so on. The two hemispheres that form the cerebrum are connected by a kind

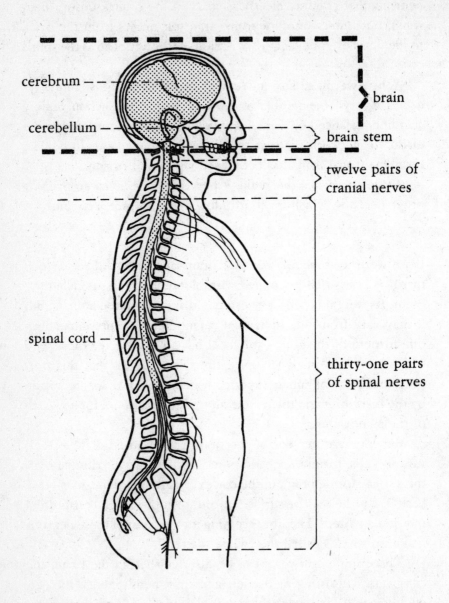

cerebrum

cerebellum

brain

brain stem

twelve pairs of
cranial nerves

spinal cord

thirty-one pairs
of spinal nerves

Figure 2—Diagram of the central nervous system

of bridge called the corpus callosum. A number of structures are located under the hemispheres (see figure 3).

How does the brain work?

For a long time, when effective means of observation and investigation were lacking, all sorts of fanciful theories about its function and operation were put forward. It was not until the early nineteenth century, with the work of Franz Joseph Gall, a German physician who was a professor in Vienna and then in Paris, that ideas on this subject became less whimsical. For research purposes, Gall collected skulls of criminals and mentally ill people, and busts of famous men. He felt the bumps and hollows of those skulls, believing that they accurately reproduced the contours of the cor-

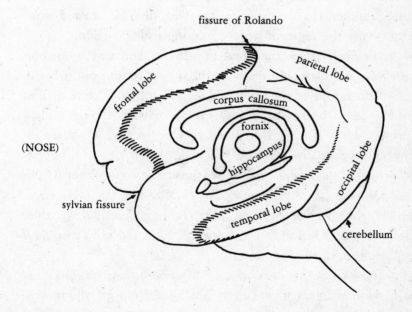

Figure 3—Diagram of the various cortical lobes

tex, the outer layer of the brain. By making comparisons between the shape of each skull he studied and what he knew about the life of the person to whom it had belonged, he developed a theory according to which each mental faculty, innate and inalterable, was produced by a specific group of nerve cells functioning in a specific location. This was the doctrine of phrenology. On the basis of it, Gall drew a kind of map of the mental faculties that was highly regarded in his time (see figures 4 and 5).

In our own time, phrenology is regarded more skeptically, to say the least. While it is true that we are all born with a certain cerebral inheritance in our genes, our faculties change under the influence of social life. Certain localizations seem odd to us, and debatable at best: it is hard to assign any scientific meaning to such terms as pride, love of authority, and love of glory. Visionary though he was, however, it is still true that Gall did the work of a pioneer by intuiting the existence of specialized regions of the brain. Along with his glaring mistakes, he sometimes made accurate judgments, as he did, for example, when he situated word memory and the sense of language in the frontal region.

Pierre-Paul Broca, the great French surgeon and anthropologist, was particularly interested in the speech centers of the brain. In 1861 he autopsied the body of an inmate of the Bicêtre asylum who had been able to speak only a single syllable, though he had expressed himself by gestures and seemed to have a certain intelligence. Broca discovered a lesion in his left frontal lobe that had probably made him unable to speak. This confirmed Gall's hypothesis, so far as that particular localization was concerned. But since the man had still been able to pronounce a single syllable, it seemed that a lesion in one specific sector did not cause *total* disappearance of the function.

We now know that the notion of ultraprecise localizations must be abandoned in favor of larger functional (sensory, motor) regions. It is also believed that the left hemisphere (in right-handed people), more specialized in the functions of writing, calculation, language, and logical thought, may have a more intuitive, inclusive apprehension of the world and may play a larger part in such ac-

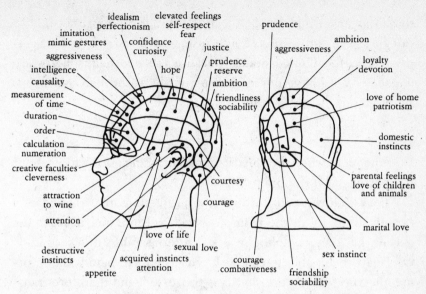

Figure 4—Phrenological map showing localizations of mental faculties as they were depicted in a work published in Gall's time. From Fonctions corticales supérieures de l'homme, *by A. R. Luria. Paris, P. U. F., 1978.*

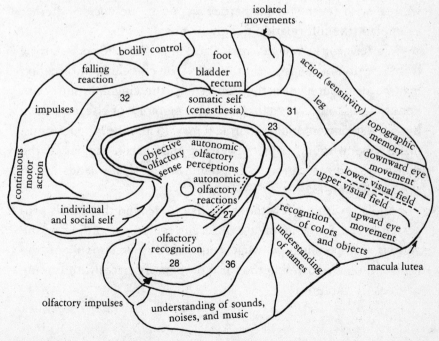

Figure 5—Map of localizations according to Kleist, 1934.

tivities as music and artistic creation, though we must not be too categorical in this area, as some researchers were for a time, especially in the United States, because the two hemispheres are connected by a large number of nerve fibers, through the corpus callosum, and work in tandem.

What happens when the electric signals bringing information about the poster reach the brain?

They follow a path through the projection areas that bears a certain similarity to the path of a steel ball in a pinball machine, except that they complete it in a few thousandths of a second.

I have been able to establish that in human beings the information conveyed by the signals is processed, and therefore transformed, in the primary regions—visual, auditory, olfactory—where they first arrive (see figures 6 and 7). Next it is compared with everything we already know about posters, and thus recognized and identified. Then, depending on the emotional charge we feel with regard to this particular poster, we decide whether to implant the information deeply or not.

We have observed that two paths may be followed: starting from a region of the frontal lobe called the cingulum, information may be distributed directly, radiated by the cingulum into both hemispheres to be stored for long-term memory; or else, especially if it has a strong emotional charge, it may go into the hippocampus, make several round trips between it and certain regions of the thalamus, and return to the cingulum, which finally sends it into the hemispheres.

And so, within a few thousandths of a second the signals processed make a trip involving different regions according to the various components of what constitutes "perception" of the poster, then are stored in the form of memory traces with varying degrees of durability.

When, voluntarily or involuntarily, we call out some of the pieces of information stored in our brain, they follow a path that is now

Figure 6—Path of signals in the brain during a memory exercise.[1]

A. *CT scan image of the brain of a young subject in a state of rest.*

B. *In the same subject during an act of memory, there is an increase in active cerebral regions (dark areas).*[2]

Figure 7

---

1. *Age et cerveau fonctionnel,* produced by Eric Duvivier, January 1986. (Festival: "Film et livre médical," photographic library of Laboratoires Fabre.)
2. *Gerontology,* 32/51/1986.

often considered to be the same as the one followed on the way in, but varying according to whether short-term or long-term memory is involved. They leave their storage site and go to their emission region, in the cortical reception regions, in the form of memories. They therefore leave where they came in. It is probably a neurotransmitter called dopamine that transports outgoing signals, as I have shown in some of my papers.

Thus looking at a poster for a few seconds, and then remembering it, brings extremely sophisticated mechanisms into play. Not only do electrical impulses and chemical substances travel at phenomenal speed along chains formed by neurons that consume glucose and oxygen, but certain interconnected regions of the brain exchange signals, store them, and take them out again at equally phenomenal speed.

At every second of our lives, even when we are asleep, as is shown by our dreams, that amazing apparatus is under tension. It never relaxes.

Now, if we consider that seeing a poster represents only a minute part of our daily cerebral activities, we realize what a marvelous machine our nervous system is—so marvelous that we are still far from knowing all its mysteries. Many questions remain. This uncertainty has given rise to many theories; some are attractive, but so far none has proved to be entirely satisfactory.

Neurophysiology still has vast territories to conquer. Its advances will probably be the great conquest of the twenty-first century.

I have used such terms as "machine," "mechanism," "electrical impulses," and "storage."

One question may occur to you: Can't the human mind be imitated, even replaced, by those famous computers with regard to which we speak of electronic memory and artificial intelligence?

Since there is a tendency nowadays to confuse science with science fiction, I think it will be useful to take our bearings in this area, and set our clocks to the right time.

The computer is a very interesting tool. Through its extraordinary quantitative performances, it makes human life easier—except when some humans use it to destroy others. It enables us to take giant steps in many realms, such as the conquest of space, for example.

But it is controlled by humans and does not create; it thinks within the limits assigned to it. The essential components of all organized thought—self-awareness, a sense of purpose, sensations, feelings, a subconscious, vital impulses—are absent from that inert structure. It is only an object, not a living being.

Moreover, in the present state of our knowledge, we cannot conceive of a computer that, after being supplied with the requisite data, could duplicate a very simple act of human creativity—like the one brought about by the sight of our poster, for example. No computer has a complexity equivalent to the number of synapses in the brain (estimated at a hundred trillion).

Maybe it will someday be possible to make a computer capable of performing that feat, assuming that there could be any reason for wanting a facsimile of an act of creativity. But the computer would probably cost a fortune and be as bulky as a building several stories high, because it would have to contain a whole system of receptors, transmitters, coders, and storage devices. Programming such a monster, and building up the associated database, would take years of work, since, as we have seen, information conveyed to the brain is of a composite nature (the image of the poster is combined with smells, sounds, sensations, moods, and so on, which must all be transformed into electronic data).

Imagine an attempt to reproduce all of someone's thoughts and memories in the course of a whole day—it would require building a city full of computers!

We differ from computers in one way that is not necessarily to our advantage: our brain system never records, stores, or gives back data as perfectly and automatically as a computer can do.

That is what we will examine next.

AN ATTENTION EXERCISE

· Can you repeat the sentence you just read at the end of this chapter? (Don't cheat. . . .)

· What is the name of the theory developed by Gall?

· What localization did he specify correctly?

· Glance at the last full page of the chapter. In thirty seconds, estimate how many words are printed on it: a hundred and fifty? three hundred? five hundred?

· Can you work out a quick and practical method for making that estimate? What is it? Are there others?

· Imagine other exercises for this chapter.

HOW YOUR BRAIN
DOES NOT WORK

The marvelous, ultrasophisticated mechanism that we have just described never works to full capacity, for several reasons.

First of all, we are not perfect creatures—nothing alive is perfect. Each of us is born with a certain number of anatomical impairments, some of which are hereditary.

Since we are thinking creatures, short-term or long-term blockages occur, caused by our emotions or our subconscious. (Without realizing it, we may *refuse* to remember a happening that we feel to be unpleasant. It may unexpectedly pop up, however, because memory sometimes plays tricks on us.)

And since we are social creatures, our cognitive system is fashioned by our cultural and emotional environment. Those lucky enough to be born into intellectual surroundings start life in an atmosphere that favors the awakening and functioning of their faculties. (But we must not exaggerate this effect: though important, it is not necessarily a determining factor.)

Finally, the various components of the mechanisms—receptors, transmitters, brain—are subject to mishaps that can be placed in three categories: the machine breaks down, malfunctions, or wears out.

With receptors, a "breakdown" is often caused by bodily accidents. The severing of an optical nerve, for example, deprives the eye of all or part of its vision; damage to an important element of the auditory apparatus may cause partial or total deafness, and so on. It is the same with neurons that transmit nerve impulses to the brain.

With the brain, there are many causes of "breakdown." Describing them all would be tedious, but a few can be noted.

A bit of fatty matter in an artery may, for various chemical and physical reasons, separate from the vascular wall and form a kind of wad which, carried along by the bloodstream, blocks an artery supplying blood to the brain, causing hemiplegia. The rupture of a blood vessel may also cause certain disorders, a tumor may put pressure on the brain, and so on.

In every case, the process is nearly the same: certain groups of neurons are deprived of their essential nourishment (oxygen and glucose) and their normal functioning is disrupted. If the deprivation does not last too long, the neurons may return to normal. Otherwise, they die. When they stop functioning, disorders appear (disorders of speech, hearing, or sensitivity, coma, epilepsy, etc.).

Sometimes, when functioning has been restored, the disorders completely disappear. Most of us have heard of people who came out of a coma and, by means of active rehabilitation, regained much or nearly all of their abilities.

But doctors also tell us something interesting on this subject: they have observed that the "return to normal" is often quicker and more successful if the patient has a resolute character. It seems that strong-willed people have a greater chance of pulling through and making up for their temporary handicaps. This is an important point and we will have occasion to come back to it. Even when neurons have died, a certain recuperation may take place.

How is it possible? Through two main mechanisms. In many brain lesions, not all of the neurons die. The lost functions may be taken over by neighboring neuron systems as a result of active rehabilitation: this is the phenomenon of cerebral functional plasticity.

In some cases, as in "normal" aging, loss of neurons is compensated for by creation of new functional junctions (by new dendrites): this is the phenomenon of structural plasticity, whose existence has been shown by many researchers.

But we must also mention a degeneration of certain groups of neurons known as Alzheimer's disease. It was formerly noted chiefly in people over seventy; it is now detected as early as the age of fifty, probably because there is much more awareness of it than before. In France there are about three hundred and fifty thousand cases of it. This represents 4.5 percent of people over sixty, so, tragic though the disease is, it affects a rather small proportion of the population.

As for malfunctions of the cerebral mechanism, there is a broad array of them.

With people who come to the institute, we begin by asking them if their sight and hearing are good, which always surprises them: they came to us because they have memory problems, and now they are being asked about their eyes and ears!

One out of three times, a quick check of those organs shows us that there is some sort of problem, from improperly fitted glasses to a hearing aid that is not worn because of misplaced vanity.

It is often in the sense organs that malfunctions take place. Let us return to the example of the poster: if, when you look at it, you have a visual weakness (which you may not be aware of because it is not troublesome), the message sent to your brain will necessarily be distorted to some extent, and of lower quality. Its other components—sounds, smells, sensation of warmth, etc.—may also be impaired.

When you look at the poster, you may have taken sleeping pills the night before. If they are taken in strong doses and repeatedly, they will eventually "dull" your sense organs, making them slower and less responsive.

Are you sure you have not taken any medicines either? Some of them cause secondary disorders in the sense organs. Read the directions carefully.

Vitamin deficiencies may adversely affect hearing or sight. Generally speaking, any pathological state diminishes the functioning of the senses. (Someone with a fever, for example, does not see and hear as well as usual.) Finally, we must mention the harmful effects—all too well known—of drugs and alcohol. Many car accidents show how much the latter distorts evaluation of distances and shapes.

Where transmission is concerned, we find the same malfunctions, with the same causes: sleeping pills, medicines, deficiencies, pathological states, alcohol and drugs perturb the metabolism of neurons, the work of neurotransmitters, or the movement of nerve impulses. The message does not travel as fast or as well.

Even so, we realize that we were not in full possession of our faculties when we transmitted and received the message. But that is far from certain. We tend to assume that our senses work perfectly and to "believe our eyes and ears." So when we question our stock of information and it gives us a vague, imprecise memory trace, we naturally conclude that we have a "bad memory."

The tragedy is that many people who have faulty sight or hearing and are not willing to correct it, or those who take too much of certain medicines or sleeping pills, come to believe, as the years go by, that they "have no memory" and, accepting it as an unavoidable and irremediable affliction, they isolate themselves from the world, cut themselves off from society, and, in a way, accelerate their own aging.

At the institute we have observed that some people begin complaining less about faulty memory when they have taken our advice to get better glasses or a hearing aid. I will not go so far as to claim that a good pair of glasses makes memory return as though by magic, but this is an aspect of the problem that should not be neglected.

As for the brain, it has malfunctions that may have the same causes as those that disturb reception and transmission. Its functioning can also be impaired by stress, anxiety, and mental illness.

Overwork may be another cause of impairment. Our brain, like the whole cerebral mechanism (and the body in general), works better when it respects a certain biological rhythm. Like an engine, it needs "overhauls" at regular intervals. If we force it to work at an abnormal rate, something similar to jet lag occurs. With jet lag, the body may be perturbed if we do not take the precaution of imposing a period of recuperation on ourselves. The cerebral equivalent of this perturbation is mental strain. Information is received, stored, and retransmitted more and more badly, and this may eventually lead to more serious disorders.

To speak of the cerebral mechanism wearing out is to raise the question of aging.

Consideration of that question is both urgent and taboo. Urgent because, thanks to progress in medical techniques, average life expectancy in Western nations has risen greatly while birth rates have remained more or less steady, which has prompted some people to predict disaster and announce that Western society's failure to renew its population will result in its gradual disappearance. Taboo because, in a society of hyperconsumption where the ideal is to be "young, suntanned, and successful," aging tends to be regarded as a failing or a serious defect.

Aging means, first of all, noticing the initial signs of physical decline. You lose your breath from climbing two flights of stairs; you can no longer play five straight sets of tennis; you begin having sore muscles or painful joints after walking a few miles; and you cannot afford to stay up as late as you used to, if you want to avoid waking up very tired the next day and having trouble working.

Aging also means looking at yourself in the mirror and noticing the first wrinkles, gray hairs, and bulges in the wrong places.

Aging, finally, means thinking that you are less attractive, and that it is no longer true that "anything is possible."

Biologically, the process of wearing out is inevitable. Our tissues and organs become less efficient with age. This also applies, of course, to the cerebral mechanism. Our senses—sight, hearing, smell, etc.—become less acute. Information is transmitted less quickly, because some neurons are less active, because enzyme exchanges, protein synthesis, and the release of neurotransmitters are slowed down, and because nerve impulses travel less rapidly.

On the subject of neurons, I would like to dispose of one persistent myth. The disorders that accompany aging are not caused by decreases in the number of neurons. It is true that we lose about a hundred thousand of them every day, which makes more than two billion between the ages of thirty and ninety—but since we start out with thirteen to fourteen billion, the loss is unimportant. Recent work has clearly shown that cerebral senescence cannot be accounted for solely by loss of neurons.

The blood-brain barrier, which protects the brain against assaults that come from the rest of the body, becomes more permeable. Certain substances, formerly blocked by that safety barrier, can now pass through it and act as poisons. And the constitution of some cerebral membranes is altered, causing them to weaken.

As we age, we become less resistant to both inner and outer assaults. We react less quickly to fewer things. But we must not overgeneralize: Verdi composed innovative operas at the age of eighty-one; Titian was past eighty when he began his *Pietà*; Picasso was in the midst of a creative period at the end of his life, and the list could go on. Not to mention the cheerful and mentally alert centenarians we sometimes see on television.

Biological aging therefore affects neither the intensity nor the nature of thought. On the contrary, some philosophies place great value on wisdom accumulated through the years, which can be attained only by venerable "masters" whose teaching is respectfully followed by their young disciples. The list is long: Socrates, Confucius . . .

At this point I can imagine an objection: "That's all very well, but how do you explain the fact that many old people are forgetful, don't recognize people they've known for years, can't deal with the details of everyday life—in other words, the fact that they become senile? It's well known!"

Yes, it is, and it deserves to be examined in depth, because what we have here is a case of extreme confusion. Serious and important though the subject is, it reminds me of a joke, as follows.

One day a graduate of the Ecole Polytechnique in Paris, a logical thinker like all graduates of that prestigious school, captured a flea and watched it closely. He shouted. The flea jumped. He cut off its legs and shouted again. The poor little insect didn't move. He concluded with scientific rigor, "If you cut off a flea's legs, it becomes deaf."

That is more or less what happens with old people. Purely physical deterioration leads to the conclusion that there has been mental deterioration as well. "My grandfather can't read anymore," it is said, because his retinas no longer enable him to see correctly. "He lives like a houseplant," because his coronary problems make certain efforts impossible for him. "His mind is going bad," because he has lapses of memory that would usually not even be noticed in a younger person, who would at most be described as "absentminded."

The fact is that someone can have a brain in perfect working order but be in bad physical condition, even bedridden, which may make others falsely believe that he or she has mental disorders. The flame of a candle provides a good comparison: even when the candle is almost entirely consumed, the flame is still the same—to someone able and willing to observe it. But not everyone is willing. Sometimes the image of a "senile" grandmother is useful in pushing her aside, no longer having to be encumbered with her, because she's such a burden. . . .

Actually, the greatest danger to old people has nothing to do with physical ailments: it comes from the social environment.

As an example, consider a man in his fifties who works. His brain system functions at a certain level (never at its maximum level, if only because, as I have pointed out, we use only a fraction of our total stock of brain cells). Then he reaches retirement age. He has been looking forward to retirement for a long time and has high hopes for it. He imagines that from now on life will be simple and easy, that he will have time to do everything he wants. And for a few months he coasts along, glad to be able to catch his breath and discover a new world.

But then things go wrong. The cerebral functions, which had

been working at a certain rate, are not called into action as much as before. The brain is like a battery that runs down if it is not used. And our retired man is like an athlete who suddenly stops training: he is soon out of condition.

During this period he feels isolated from his family and his work environment: his children have married and made lives of their own, his former colleagues are also going off into retirement, and he finds himself alone. A kind of break takes place. He has the feeling that he is no longer participating in the life of society, that he is not useful to anyone or anything, that he is "outside." He still has to organize his own life. His occupational world was governed by rules, and although they were restrictive, they assured that everyone was always defined, rooted, and protected within a whole. Now that those barriers are gone, no path is marked out before him, and he is more disquieted than attracted by the vast horizon that has suddenly opened to him.

The first reaction in this situation is usually to turn inward and close oneself to the world, which makes one even more "out of condition." The less we ask of our brain, the less it gives us, and eventually there are signs of what I call cerebral hypoefficiency: memory difficulties; absentmindedness; little quirks; inability to handle certain details of everyday life, such as using a household appliance or organizing a shopping trip to several different stores.

Sometimes hypoefficiency goes no further than that, but often, unfortunately, it worsens and leads people afflicted with it to ask for more and more help from others—that is, to become dependent just when others are moving away from them.

To come back to the example of our retired man, suppose he decides that rather than asking for help from his relatives, he will try to solve his problems on his own. What should he do? First, go to see his doctor. Until recently, the doctor would usually have said something like this: "You're forgetful and you feel that your mind is deteriorating? Don't worry, that's perfectly normal: it's only age." Giving up and drifting into a life of inferior quality was (and too often still is) regarded as a sensible response to an inevitable situation. And that attitude was reflected by the aging person's family: "Look, it's only natural for you to have all those little problems. It's because of your age and there's nothing you can do about it."

But if our retired man, refusing to give up and accept his hypoefficiency as inescapable, decides to stand on his own two feet and take full responsibility for himself, what is he offered?

Historically, treatment of the elderly has gone through different phases.

At first they remained within the family, where they fulfilled an educational function as transmitters of tradition. They were respected as such, and there was nothing derogatory about the word "old"; on the contrary, it was a synonym of "wise."

Then economic constraints—housing shortages, the high cost of living, etc.—made old people become an increasingly heavy burden for the nuclear family, which reacted by trying to get rid of them. Public and private "homes" for them sprang up like mushrooms. There they were given "complete care," which actually meant placing them in a state of total inaction, and only accelerated the process of senility.

We are now coming into a third phase, not because society or the family has suddenly taken a keen interest in the elderly's fate, but because their increasing number has made it apparent that they form a large market. And gerontology has proven to be a lucrative field.

The current trend is to place them in groups and offer them "leisure activities."

I doubt that being penned up and seeing only other people in their declining years is the best solution. We have gone from the asylum to the corral. I believe that old people should go on living in contact with people of all ages.

As for the "leisure activities" offered to the elderly, they generally do not really take part in them: they are more often passive spectators than active participants. Many old people have talked to me on that subject, and I must say it is sometimes rather depressing. So many endless lectures during which they fall asleep! They do not participate in the world: the spectacle of the world is imposed on them.

We must quickly enter a new phase, one in which the elderly, unwilling to play the game and serve the interests of those in the "old age business," take themselves in hand, refuse to consider themselves excluded from society, and live their lives fully and totally without owing anything to anyone.

Brain Fitness is a means they can use to get out of their ghetto and achieve an independence that is accessible to them, provided they really want it.

AN ATTENTION EXERCISE

· Without looking at it again, estimate the number of lines there are on the last full page of this chapter: more than twenty, more than thirty, fewer than thirty?

· Now look back at that page, pencil in hand, and draw a line through all the n's you see, as quickly as you can. As soon as you finish, say how many you found.

· What are the substances that neurons need for their nutrition?

· How many neurons do we lose between the ages of thirty and ninety?

· Write a brief definition of cerebral hypoefficiency:

Check to see if your answers are correct.

THE BIRTH OF
BRAIN FITNESS

Briefly summarizing the results of years spent elaborating hypotheses, doing research, and carrying out experiments is a real challenge, but I have tried to meet it. I ask my readers to forgive my occasional lapses into scientific jargon; I have done my best to weed it out as often as possible, but unfortunately it is sometimes unavoidable.

Since all scientific work involves a certain amount of human adventure, I have chosen to mingle a few elements of my own life with the story of my research. I think it will make my account more vivid and accessible.

I hope my readers will follow the various stages of my journey with the same curiosity and interest I felt at the time. They will have the advantage of traveling in conquered territory and therefore not having to go through the periods of doubt and sometimes discouragement that researchers often encounter.

THE LABORATORY

I was almost born in the midst of test tubes. My father, a veterinarian (he is now retired), divided his time between laboratory research and the animals he took care of in the Breton countryside. He headed one of the first French artificial insemination centers for cattle and contributed greatly to its development.

Steeped in that atmosphere, I decisively announced my vocation at an early age: I would be a Pasteur or nothing. That great scientist's discoveries filled me with wonder, and my heart was stirred when I read the moving story of the Alsatian boy he saved from rabies.

At the same time, there was another factor that, without my knowing it then, would determine my future career. Being an only child and a little solitary by nature, I particularly liked the company of adults, especially old people. I felt at ease with them; they pampered me and told me good stories. Those old people of rural Brittany were often real forces of nature and had prodigious memories. I regarded them as fully developed adults. To the child I was then, they represented the strength and majesty of grownups at a time when family ties and social conviviality still allowed them to play a full part in life. Sometimes I also encountered sick people, young or old, but it would never have occurred to me that there might be a connection between being handicapped or in poor health and being old: they were—and still are—two different things.

Though I had a burning desire to be a scientist, I also had a curious, open mind that departed a little from what was considered to be scientific rigor. Mathematics was said to be vitally important, but it bored me. I preferred philosophy, not as a source of concepts, but as a "mechanism of thought." I have always liked to take clocks apart.

After graduating from high school I should logically have gone to medical school, but I wasn't charmed by the prospect of spending the rest of my life treating sore throats and setting fractures. (I hope my medical friends and collaborators will excuse that rather harsh view of their profession.) To tell the truth, no career really attracted me, and, not knowing where else to go, I ended up in law school at Rouen. I went there with the idea that, after all, law was a field where mental effort did not wander off into abstractions, but led to concrete reality. To my dismay, however, I had to swallow tons of law books that seemed to me more and more indigestible.

As luck would have it (and luck often has the right idea), psychology classes were taught in the building next to the one where I was wasting away. In their final year, students there could work toward a certificate in neurophysiology.

Blithely skipping my law classes, I soon became keenly interested in that new field, where the "how it works" of the brain was taught from a much wider perspective than the purely medical approach.

Jean Charpentier, the professor in charge of study toward the certificate, was a psychopharmacology enthusiast. He quickly infected me with his virus and I joined the team he was forming to carry on experimental studies, in the laboratory, of the behavior of animals under the influence of certain substances, particularly soporifics.

It did not take me long to realize that I had found my way. I undertook a third-stage thesis on memory disorders, especially those related to hypoxia, that is, oxygen deficiency in neurons, which must consume a certain amount of oxygen to continue functioning. What interested me was determining the biochemical mechanisms in the brain that caused memory disorders in animals given an inadequate supply of oxygen.

With my third-stage doctorate in my pocket, I worked as a laboratory assistant at the medical school in Rouen, where Professor Francis Boismare taught pharmacology and also hemodynamics, that is, the study of blood circulation, particularly, in this case, circulation through the cerebral arteries. At the same time, I continued my experiments on memory.

Things were going well for me. I was enriching my knowledge, accumulating theories, collecting observations. A career was laid out before me: I could join a team doing advanced basic research and then, in a little world cut off from others (everything was, and still is, done within isolated groups), I would take part in a kind of sequestered competition *against* other teams. With a little luck, I could someday announce in a specialized publication that I had succeeded in refuting the theories of a rival coterie.

I was not tempted by such a future. Purely theoretical research did not satisfy me. I wanted to *see* how things really worked in the brain—that was the "taking clocks apart" side of me. At that time, however, imaging techniques were only at the beginning of their development, so I was left with a feeling of frustration. But above all I had the feeling that nothing of what was being presented to me had any connection with reality. How did it concern people who suffered from memory difficulties? No one else seemed to care about them, but I wanted to help them, give them something—that was the "Pasteur" side of me.

Then luck smiled on me again. While I was working on an eight-year state doctorate at the Saint-Antoine hospital in Paris and teaching at the school of pharmacy in Dijon, I met Professor Jean-Robert Rapin, a radiopharmacologist who introduced me to radioisotopes. At last I could actually *see* brain activity in an animal!

Radioisotopes are substances (radioactive tracers) that are injected into an animal and, according to their characteristics, become fixed in one part or another of the brain. There they emit radiation that makes it possible to observe what is taking place. Previously, the study of brain functioning was hindered by the fact that the blood-brain barrier blocked the passage of substances intended for observation. When I began working with radioisotopes, they were known but were not commonly or systematically used in animal experimentation.

They were a real revelation to me. Now I could see how blood was distributed in the brain, how neurons consumed their glucose and oxygen—and therefore expended energy, and therefore *worked*.

That wonderful tool of observation I had at my disposal gave me an idea: I could teach certain kinds of behavior to laboratory animals, *visualize* what took place in their brains, and form a kind of image that I will call a functional map. Maybe I could find out, by means of radioactive tracers, which regions worked actively, or less actively, or not at all, in response to the demand for certain kinds of effort. If so, I would have the great advantage of being able to quickly observe the effect of a manipulation on the brain, then reproduce that observation at will and determine whether some of my hypotheses were right or wrong.

I went to work.

In the course of my observations I made some discoveries that seemed important to me. If we observe the functional map of an animal not engaged in any specific activity, it gives us a certain image, a "rest image," which corresponds to the fact that the animal's neurons are working at a reduced rate. If the animal is made to go through a maze to get food, we see that the map is altered. Certain groups of neurons whose metabolism was previously at a low level have now gone to work. If we demand another task of our animal, we get still another image.

We may conclude that a different image, and therefore an activation of different neurons, corresponds to each effort. But each group of neurons does not work in isolation. Everything is done in interaction: different groups take part in a single task, in varying degrees. I have never been able to observe a *unique* memory center, for example. Extreme localization has therefore never seemed to me an obvious fact, because I have never had visual evidence of it, even though some researchers still maintain that it exists.

Another discovery that seemed important to me was the part played by the animal's age. I was able to determine that, for a specific task, an old rat (twenty-two months) and a young one (four months) activated comparable areas of neurons, though the activation sometimes took longer in the old one. But if the old one was specially trained, he performed the same as the young one. His functional map showed that the number of active neurons had increased.

The essential point is that a rat of any age can be made to activate more neurons, and therefore to extend his areas of cerebral activity, simply by progressively putting him through a certain number of exercises. He must *want* to do them, however. To bring that about, he is motivated; in this case, he must find his food or water, which has been placed in a certain part of the maze, or will be delivered to him only if he solves certain problems or performs certain acts. We go from the simplest to the most complicated.

Let us take two very hungry rats and confront them with a rather complex problem of obtaining food. The first one, untrained, will quickly lose his motivation, give up trying to solve the problem, and die of hunger, sometimes a few inches away from the food. The second one, having been trained, will eventually find the way to obtain the food.

How have things happened within the brain? Here again, the image enables us to answer.

As I have said, only a fraction of our neurons function. About eighty percent of them are unused; these are quiescent neurons, which are not made for this particular task. They are simply there, under tension, like a team's substitutes watching the game.

In some of my experiments* I have established a number of important facts.

---

* IPA Psychogeriatrics Congress, Chicago, August 1987.

When a rat is subjected to training, it can be seen from the functional map of his brain that his quiescent neurons gradually awaken and their metabolism increases. There is a greater quantity of neurotransmitters released, in an activation that spreads from cell to cell. The substitutes have left their bench and joined in the game; the areas of active neurons have been extended.

But things may go much further.

What happens if damage is inflicted on certain areas of active neurons in a rat that is able to solve the problems set for him in the maze? Unable to perform as he did before, he becomes inactive. He can expect no help from his own body; he is doomed. But if he is trained to perform certain new acts (reaching a baby bottle to obtain water, for example), this training soon bears fruit: he relearns the forgotten act. The bottle is placed very close to him at first, then gradually moved farther away; he passes from the very easy to the more difficult.

What has happened? A neuronal area near the damaged one has been recruited; or, to resume the sporting comparison, a team that had to leave the field has been replaced by another, which, like the first one, was originally not highly specialized and had to be trained to make it capable of playing effectively.

This phenomenon is known in neurophysiology as neural functional plasticity. We have already spoken of structural plasticity. What is the difference between the two phenomena? In structural plasticity, the neuron remains alive, and new dendrites are developed when active retraining is carried out. We can say that everything grows back from the cell body, which acts like the trunk of a tree whose branches have been cut off: it sends out sap and its branches grow again. In functional plasticity, however, the neuron is dead. The tree is no longer usable, and nearby trees are used instead.

In the first case, retraining permits resumption of the lost function. In the second, the replacement neuron, which previously played no part in the lost function, must be taught its new work. The brain must be put through "mental gymnastics."

When an accident happens, it causes both limited lesions,

which do not affect the cell body, and more serious ones that kill certain groups of neurons. So retraining methods borrow from both of the organism's systems of defense, which, let me emphasize, can come into play only if the injured person intervenes to guide that reconquest by performing appropriate exercises.

I recently placed rats in a situation where a source of water was accessible only with difficulty, and I ascertained that even if they were very thirsty they rapidly lost their motivation: they stopped moving and seemed overwhelmed with fatigue. The older they were, the more quickly they lost their motivation.* When I examined their brain maps I saw that, whether they were young or old, there was deterioration of whole areas of neurons, notably in the hippocampus.

It is an instructive discovery: no matter what his age, but especially if he is old, a rat's brain deteriorates if he is placed in conditions that cause him to lose motivation, so that he apparently no longer has any desire to eat or drink, and therefore to live. I did not bring about the deterioration by creating a lesion in the animal, but simply by changing his psychic conditions.

I also observed that if I moved water or food close to the rat *before* lesions appeared, I activated his reactions and he totally regained his cerebral functioning. This may mean that psychic conditions play an important part in deterioration of the animal's brain: they may provide fertile ground for it.

My experiments thus suggested that certain types of degeneration might be prevented by changing psychic conditions as soon as possible. One question came into my mind very early in the course of those experiments: How could those purely experimental discoveries be taken out of the laboratory and applied to people?

---

* *Ibid.*

PEOPLE

The idea of promoting a program designed for people with degenerative diseases would never have occurred to me, even though—and I will return to this—I had come to a number of conclusions on the subject.

I was certain, however, that something significant could be done here and now for people with nonpathological cerebral problems such as memory failures, absentmindedness, and difficulties in adjusting to the intrusive technology of modern life, for all those people, no matter what their age, who felt a little disoriented and "out of tune" with the world around them, and who were imperturbably told that it was "normal"—so normal that nothing could be done for them.

I was also convinced that those problems should be treated very soon after their onset or, if possible, preventively, before they appeared.

I still had to find a method.

I knew what I wanted to do: stimulate those people's cerebral functioning by activating their "silent regions," where neurons were quiescent, unused. Those groups of neurons had to be put to work. The people would then improve their performances, stop being buffeted by the difficulties of everyday life, and solve a large part of their practical problems. And, being better adjusted, they would probably have more pleasant lives.

What I did not yet know was *how* I was going to do that.

Create a method of cerebral activation? Yes, but what form should it take?

I was no longer dealing with laboratory animals, but with my fellow humans. Should I simply "unload" my experience on them, tell them what to do, give them step-by-step instructions? I felt that would lead to failure.

I preferred to begin by devoting several months to practical investigation. I met with leaders and members of clubs for old people, and with medical specialists—neurologists, psychiatrists, geriatricians—as well as general practitioners, particularly Dr. Jamot, my family doctor, with whom I had long discussions and spent a great deal of time going through medical records.

A number of constants gradually became apparent to me.

Generally speaking, two attitudes toward old age can be discerned. First, there are those who regard it as a purely physical problem and treat it as such: they go on living more or less as they did in their younger days, and, while they suffer from the biological effects of age, their minds are as clear as ever and function perfectly. The old people who enchanted me in my childhood undoubtedly belonged to this category.

Then there is the second attitude, which, unfortunately, is more widespread: lack of motivation. It is usually brought on, as we have seen, by retirement, which first produces a social break, then has serious family and, finally, psychological consequences, in a process that may be compared to fuses blowing out one after another. One feels *shoved aside*, then *lonely*, then *old*. This chain reaction gradually leads to cerebral hypoefficiency. It is not the other way around; that is, it is not because some of their neurons become quiescent and gaps appear in their memories that older people sink into sadness, withdraw from the world, and, in general, behave as if they had been defeated by life. The opposite is true: it is because they are psychologically weak, suffer from loneliness and despondency, and lose their motivation, that regions of their brains eventually become quiescent. It thus seems that morale is all-important.

I realized that in this respect people were their own worst enemies. They were convinced from the start that their age excluded them from this or that activity. They reasoned as follows: "Since my eyes aren't as good as they were, and I'm losing my hair, and my skin is less smooth, and I can't run as fast as I could when I was younger, it's only natural that my mind doesn't work as well as it used to." To that I answered, "As far as your eyes, hair, skin, and legs are concerned, you don't have any extra ones in reserve, but even at your age a large part of your brain cells aren't being used. You're lucky that your mind still has great possibilities." But I failed to shake their conviction.

Furthermore, I met old people who were greatly concerned about their appearance (which is commendable), had their faces lifted, used sunlamps to give themselves an artificial tan, or fell prey to "youth merchants" who sold them all sorts of wondrous nostrums and treatments, yet were skeptical or suspicious when I told them they could preserve their mental abilities at less expense.

I then went on to the next stage. When people told me that their memory was "going bad," I suggested the exercises I was developing. It was all empirical, of course; I was still groping. I based that work primarily on speed of reaction.

It finally became apparent to me, and to the people doing the exercises, that their mental agility was returning at a spectacular rate. And this had a beneficial effect on their whole outlook. They stopped behaving like victims and tended to take charge of their own lives to a greater extent. This was not always the case, of course, and the process took time, but as I developed and refined my methods I had the satisfaction of seeing the percentage of successes increase.

Another constant appeared to me at the end of my investigation: nothing can succeed without motivation. Take the example of a thirsty rat who, faced with a difficulty too great for him, stops moving and no longer makes any effort to reach the water that will save him. Even if he is bombarded with external stimuli—electric currents, etc.—he will remain in that helpless state. But if the water is brought close enough to him while he continues to be stimulated, he will come out of his torpor and make the effort of going to drink. With all due allowance, it is the same with human beings: to get them to activate their brains, one must explain the why and the how of the exercises, and activation is possible only if it coincides with their desire for improvement. It is they who will ask the brain to activate quiescent groups of neurons, and it is to them that the brain will respond.

That is why it became clear to me very early that the method I was going to develop would depend to a large extent on each person's conscientiousness and will. And it is also why a good part of this book is devoted to describing the cerebral mechanism, even though it may sometimes seem a little tedious.

At the beginning of this chapter I said that the method I had developed was not meant for people with degenerative diseases, but it may be remembered that I had noted the appearance of degeneration in the course of my laboratory experiments. If, for example, we examine the brain map of a rat who has lost motivation, remains inert, and will no longer make the effort of trying to reach water, we see, whether he is young or old, that it shows areas of degeneration. But if he is remotivated before those lesions appear, if he is sufficiently activated, his brain map shows no such lesions.

So I thought it might be possible to prevent certain types of degeneration. That was only a hypothesis. I discussed it at length with the specialists I encountered in the course of my investigation. Some of them thought I was mistaken, that the phenomena of cerebral degeneration were caused by heredity; others said they were related to certain toxic substances; still others linked them to a virus. But, unfortunately, those theories were all unverified, and none of them seemed to me more convincing than my own.

I was not, however, in a position to state positively that I was right. Though Dr. Jamot and I had observed that people who practiced my method made rapid progress, I had no way of proving that a nonfunctional brain degenerated more quickly; in other words, that neurons died from being quiescent too long. Nor could I claim—I had no statistical proof—that my method made it possible to work effectively against certain types of degeneration.

I had the main elements of an effective method for combating cerebral hypoefficiency, and I wanted to try to verify my theory about degeneration. I now had to find a framework in which I could put my methods into practice and conduct research on both animals and human beings.

For administrative and budgetary reasons, a university would not lend itself to my purpose. To me, organizations for basic and applied research had the serious drawback of not being willing enough to rub up against reality. They have not changed much: in my opinion, they still suffer from that same drawback. At a recent meeting in Canada I suggested to several British and American researchers the idea of an institution in which various countries could compare their views on the problem of cerebral aging; subjects for research could then be worked out on the basis of guidelines applicable to all the countries involved. My distinguished colleagues looked at me in surprise. Why should they work together like that? They were already carrying on their own research, each in his own way, and that was enough. I insistently pointed out that while they were off in their separate corners, absorbed in their own work, old people were going through real tragedies, abandoned by everyone. They shrugged that off: "Taking care of old people isn't our job. It's a political problem."

I concluded that there was no framework corresponding to what I was looking for. I would have to invent one.

THE INSTITUTE

The INRPVC (Institut National de Recherche sur la Prévention du Vieillissement Cérébral: National Institute for Research on the Prevention of Cerebral Aging) was founded in 1984. It was housed on the premises of Public Assistance at the Bicêtre hospital, but was governed and financed by an independent association.

My goal, which many were sure I would never reach, was to create a basic research organization that would not only lead to applied research, but would also attack a national problem: the cerebral aging of the population. It was a vast program! We might have been accused of trying to marry fire and water when we set up working relations between researchers and technicians, "eggheads" and adminstrators, who are known to be strongly allergic to each other in France.

We began small, not out of modesty, but because our financial means were severely limited. (They still are, unfortunately, and sometimes making both ends meet is a hazardous feat, as it was in the heroic early days.)

Researchers belonging to multidisciplinary teams now work at the institute: physicians, chemists, psychologists, and computer specialists compare their work and exchange ideas, in coordination with teams of physicians working in the field.

Every day, at Bicêtre and the various regional centers* that our association has created in France, we receive men and women who have, or are on the verge of having, problems of cerebral hypoefficiency.**

The institute functions like a three-stage rocket.

To the people who come to us, either of their own accord or on their doctors' advice, we first propose a CRA (Cerebral Resources Assessment) intended primarily to determine whether or not they unknowingly have any organic brain disorders. It explores their cognitive functions (verbal, visuospatial, logical, associative, and psychomotor abilities) and makes it possible to take stock of their cerebral abilities. Its purpose is not at all to provide any sort of intelligence quotient.

The results of the various CRA's taken at the institute or our regional centers are fed into a database that is constantly kept up to date. This database has led us to some important clinical and psychosociological conclusions. First of all, contrary to a widespread opinion, people are capable of good cerebral efficiency regardless of their age. Eighteen percent are remarkably efficient and their medical history (as reported by their usual doctors) reveals no operations or disorders such as diabetes and high blood pressure. Twenty-one percent reach the age bracket of seventy to seventy-five with perfectly satisfactory cerebral efficiency, but with joint disease, high blood pressure, weakened sight or hearing, diabetes, etc. Four and a half percent show symptoms of degenerative disease. This database is highly important because it represents a typical aging process for the whole population, in relation to age brackets and sociocultural levels.

Everyone who takes a CRA is compared with the average for people of his or her sociocultural level and age bracket, with no history of medical problems. In this way we have singled out 57

---

* A list of these centers can be obtained from the INRPVC.

** The institute can now provide general practitioners with a computerized "neuromnemonic assessment" that will permit early detection of patients who have a brain disorder or are at risk of developing one.

percent of those taking CRA's who can be said to be hypoefficient because they are below the average for their age bracket and sociocultural level. Recent preliminary work has confirmed that in everyday living the link between lack of motivation and cerebral hypoefficiency appears quite clearly.*

These hypoefficient people show no brain lesions, only a kind of abnegation. "I'm old," they say, "I don't enjoy anything, my memory is going bad," and so on.

With such people it is quite possible to overcome deficiencies related to hypoefficiency. To help them "turn themselves around," we have them do exercises in groups led by psychologists: this is Brain Fitness, which uses various cognitive activities, including memory exercises.

Very soon, after only a month, it became apparent to us that these people were showing a psychological improvement: they realized that they had no real memory disorders, but were simply not really integrated into their environment, and they quickly regained good efficiency. Then, even at the age of seventy or seventy-five, they quickly regained confidence in their cerebral future.

We were able to show the efficacy of Brain Fitness statistically, in individual cases before and after the method, and collectively, in a group of 357 subjects (see figure 8).

The second stage of the rocket uses techniques of nuclear medicine.

As I have said, radioisotopes enabled me to see how groups of neurons in a rat's brain were activated in relation to cerebral activity. By means of a motion picture camera that moves around the patient's head, nuclear medicine makes it possible to determine the degree of activity of neuron groups in the human brain. We can clearly see the differences that exist in young or old subjects

---

* Naudra Arvay, *Contributions à l'étude de la plainte mnésique du sujet âgé,* medical thesis, Université Paris VI, Faculté Salpétrière, September 1987. To be published in C. Derouesné, N. Arvay, P. Migeon, M. Vollant, A. Alperovitch, and M. Le Poncin, *Memory Complaints in the Elderly.*

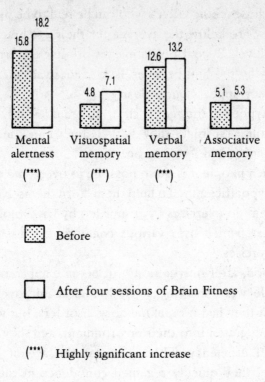

Figure 8—Changes in the performances of 357 subjects before and after Brain Fitness

with normal efficiency (figure 9, A and B) or hypoefficiency (C), and we can visualize the degeneration typical of Alzheimer's disease (D).

We can also show the efficacy of Brain Fitness in reactivating groups of neurons that had been quiescent (figure 10). Computerized tomography gives us a new look at the brain.

Each of us has a "brainprint" that, like a fingerprint, is different from all others in the world. It is constituted by the various regions of active and inactive neurons.

The final image of this kind is formed by superimposing several different images. We all have a basic stock of active neurons that

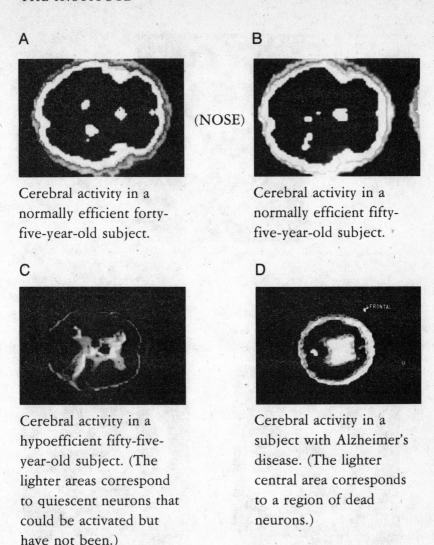

A

Cerebral activity in a normally efficient forty-five-year-old subject.

(NOSE)

B

Cerebral activity in a normally efficient fifty-five-year-old subject.

C

Cerebral activity in a hypoefficient fifty-five-year-old subject. (The lighter areas correspond to quiescent neurons that could be activated but have not been.)

D

Cerebral activity in a subject with Alzheimer's disease. (The lighter central area corresponds to a region of dead neurons.)

Figure 9—Imaging of cerebral regions by CT scan

enable us to survive: they take precedence when we want to drink, eat, walk, etc. This is what I will call the first stock, and it varies rather little from one individual to another. The second one is fashioned by occupational activities, and since a mathematician and a pastry cook, for example, do not use the same groups of neurons in their work, this stock shows a greater variation in different

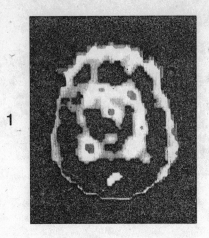

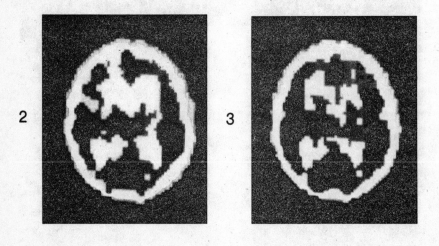

Figure 10—Before and after Brain Fitness: passage from cerebral quiescence to activity. CT scans of a hypoefficient patient (1), then after a month of cerebral activation (2), and finally after three months (3), showing a resumption of activity in formerly quiescent groups of neurons (passage from light color {cerebral quiescence} to dark color {activity}).

individuals. The third one is even more specific: it varies with our leisure activities, the sports we practice, our tastes, our creative endeavors.

The "brainprint" usually finishes taking on its general form between the ages of twenty-five and twenty-eight. Even after that, however, it can still change for the worse or for the better. For the worse: groups of neurons are damaged by a "breakdown" or a "malfunction," or lack of motivation produces quiescent regions of varying size. For the better: Brain Fitness makes it possible to reactivate quiescent regions.

And here I am thinking not only of people who suffer from hypoefficiency.

In their work, most people are specialists of one kind or another. They therefore activate certain regions of the brain to the detriment of others, which remain quiescent. As long as problems find their solutions in familiar behaviors (this is called monostrategy), things go very well. But if we are confronted with problems of a new kind, we have great difficulty in activating the quiescent regions.

Because it develops exercises of different styles that call on our multiple faculties, Brain Fitness gives rise to multistrategies that make it possible to cope with difficulties when they arise, and, more generally, to increase our cerebral efficiency in daily life.

Now for the third stage of the rocket.

We are all exposed to the risk of an injury or a stroke that can cause a massive loss of neurons and therefore a serious disturbance of the cognitive functions. People who have practiced Brain Fitness can recruit large groups of neurons in a more harmonious way; because of the diversity of that technique, their neuron groups are at work "all over," in various parts of the brain. Functional neuroplasticity—that is, the ability of nonspecialized neurons to become activated and take over—will then be greater and more rapid.

I am convinced that this advantage exists, and my belief is reinforced every day by studies that we conduct in collaboration with the medical profession. From a purely statistical standpoint, however, it has not yet been proved in an obvious, irrefutable, and official way. We will have to wait several years for that. The number of cases observed will have to be large enough to make what is still only a scientific hypothesis become recognized as a certainty.

But in the meantime, what attitude should we take toward people who ask us if Brain Fitness can enable them to react better if they have a cerebral lesion?

To answer no would be contrary to our conviction, which is strengthened by the cases we have examined. To answer yes might seem too categorical, since our conviction does not yet have an unquestionable statistical basis. What we do, then, is to tell them that they are dealing with a version of "Pascal's wager." If they practice Brain Fitness they can gain cerebral autonomy more easily; of that we are certain. Their cognitive functions will work better and faster, which will enable them to solve many psychological and social problems. They also will have a certain probability of making a better recovery in case of brain damage. What do they have to lose?

This "wager" can also be extended to the last stage of the rocket. At the institute we are now studying the degenerative Alzheimer's disease, which I have already mentioned. We believe that groups of unused neurons that have remained quiescent too long may degenerate more rapidly and thus be a cause of this type of disease, or at least provide favorable conditions for its onset, and that properly conducted activation may prevent it. But, again, only the future can prove or disprove our belief.*

To begin doing Brain Fitness is to struggle against that kind of problem, which may be partly caused by cerebral underactivity, and in the long run it is a way of betting on the future.

---

* M. Le Poncin, J. R. Rapin, J. Sotton, and C. Derouesné, "L'Hypo-efficience: porte d'entreé des maladies dégénératives?," January 1987, Laboratoires UCB.

A MONTH OF
PRACTICE

The purpose of the activation we are going to practice for four weeks is to make our cerebral capacities rapidly reactive to the many tasks that will be presented to them: we are going to learn to react *quickly*.

We will activate a greater number of neuronal circuits by performing diverse tasks. We will thus adapt ourselves to the highly varied information reaching us and learn to react "on all fronts."

Speed and diversification: both are necessary, and they must be developed together.

Since this will require concentration, the exercises must be done under the best possible psychological conditions. Don't even try to do Brain Fitness when you are upset, or if you have family problems to solve (taking care of the children, for example), or, in general, at times when your mind would not be fully focused on the exercises. And it would be pointless to do them during periods of anxiety or depression: the results would be distorted and your effort would be wasted.

I therefore think that before going on to the exercises themselves, it will be useful for you to make a preliminary assessment. Here are two questionnaires,* one devoted to anxiety, the other

---

* *Ibid.*

to depression, which I ask you to fill out by marking all questions to which your answer is yes—as honestly as possible, of course:

FIRST QUESTIONNAIRE

1. Are you feeling more nervous and anxious than usual? ☐

2. Do you sometimes feel afraid for no reason? ☐

3. Are you easily annoyed? ☐

4. Are you bothered by stomachaches, or pains in your back or neck? ☐

5. Do you sometimes feel as if you are about to faint? ☐

6. Do you have trouble falling asleep, and do you feel tired when you wake up? ☐

7. Do you have nightmares? ☐

SECOND QUESTIONNAIRE

1. Do you feel melancholy and sad, and not in the mood for doing anything? ☐

2. Do you feel less energetic than you used to when you get up in the morning? ☐

3. Do you sometimes cry, or feel like crying? ☐

4. Are you as interested as ever in your everyday activities, and are they still as easy for you? ☐

5. Do you have difficulty in making decisions? ☐

6. Do you have the feeling of not being very useful? ☐

If you marked five or more questions in each of the two questionnaires, it does not necessarily mean that you are extremely anxious or depressed, but it would be useful for you to consider the possible effect of these states of mind on your performance of Brain Fitness.

The month of practice that I am proposing to you is divided into three activation sessions per week, each lasting no more than fifteen minutes, to be carried out preferably in the morning or late afternoon, in a calm, quiet place. Never right after a meal or physical exertion, and always when you can give the exercises your full attention.

A very important point: stick closely to the observation time indicated for each exercise. And you should, of course, answer as quickly as possible. A maximum time is given for answering each question. Try not to go beyond it, checking yourself with a stopwatch.

When you begin doing the exercises you will have some successes, and also some failures. The failures will be useful to you, since they will let you know which mental capacities you most need to improve; the weakest ones will often be the least used. You will develop them in particular, and you will discover that you can quickly make up for your deficiencies and become competent in areas you had thought to be beyond your ability. You will see that anything is possible when determination is combined with technique.

If you sometimes feel discouraged, remind yourself that you are starting from the bottom and will necessarily make progress. But remember that your efforts will be effective only if you make a total commitment. So don't let yourself be disheartened! Be tenacious; try to answer every question, even if you have to go back over some of the exercises repeatedly, and look at the right answers only if you have failed several times.

A few "tricks" will help you to succeed. They are based on the associative principle and strategic mobility.

THE ASSOCIATIVE PRINCIPLE

This is a method of fixing something in your memory by associating it with an already known point of reference; that is, in practicing "associations of ideas." For example, if you want to remember a color, you can think of a garment belonging to you, or someone you know, which has that color. There are many possible references, of course, and it is up to everyone to find his or her own trick. A date can be linked not only to another date, but also to a telephone number or a street address; a person's name can be linked to all or part of another name, or an adjective, and so on.

This coupling of the new with the old, of the nonmemorized with the memorized, is already a beneficial form of fitness, because sometimes we must rack our brains to find the point of association. Furthermore, it makes memorization not only easier, but also stronger. You will find that with time this technique becomes quicker and more refined: you will make associations more rapidly and easily.

STRATEGIC MOBILITY

In the various activities of life, especially work, each of us uses a certain strategy by preference, because it is the most effective and profitable, and quite logically—or so we believe, at least—we do not change it. In this we are like a child who piles chairs on top of one another and climbs up on them to reach a jar of jam at the top of a cupboard: if that method works, why change it?

The trouble is that as time goes by we tend to favor that strategy more and more, no matter what the circumstances, out of habit or mental laziness. We are then in the position of our jam-loving child when, wanting to reach the jar, he discovers that there are no more chairs: he is disoriented and will think only much later, if ever, of going to get a ladder from the basement. Similarly, some executives or business owners, faced with difficulties or new developments in the market, cannot (or will not) make the effort of giving up their old strategies and finding new ones: their thought processes have "stiffened up." This lack of mental flexibility often leads to failure.

So when you encounter a problem in the course of the exercises, don't automatically reason according to your usual strategy, but be flexible and try to find another way. It will be even better if you come back to some of the exercises to see, just for fun, if you can find a different method of solving them.

The program of exercises presented here is based on five types of activities:

PERCEPTIVE ACTIVITY

The goal is to train and develop your perceptive ability. We have seen the importance of rapid and precise perception of information. You should therefore train your senses of sight, hearing, smell, and touch for speed as well as acuteness and discrimination.

VISUOSPATIAL ACTIVITY

This deals with information involving both sight and space. The term "space" includes the notions of location, area, volume, distance, interval, and orientation.

STRUCTURALIZATION ACTIVITY

Structuralization implies construction. The idea is to develop your ability to build a structure from individual elements. You must consider how the different pieces of information are organized, fitted together, and regrouped in order to form a coherent whole.

LOGICAL ACTIVITY

This uses arguments, reasoning, and deductions. You must find the logical sequence of certain elements and thus discover the coherence of an idea or a situation.

VERBAL ACTIVITY

This requires use of the right words (spoken or written) to define an object, an idea, an act, or a concept. It may be a visual-verbal activity that involves sight, an aural-verbal activity that involves hearing, or a conceptual activity that leads to a more abstract representation of a person, relation, or situation.

Finally, you will exercise your short-term memory and your long-term memory.

When you have sat down in a quiet place, in favorable surroundings, with a pencil and a watch, about to start doing exercises that you should regard not as onerous work, but as training to make your brain more efficient, you will be like a pianist who has sat down to practice a certain number of scales and arpeggios according to a specific plan. He knows that he must impose some constraints on himself, but that their purpose is to make his playing livelier, nimbler, and more fluid. When he has acquired that practice, he will be able to achieve a certain technical mastery, and it alone will enable him to give free rein to his temperament or his inspiration.

Similarly, by freeing you from the hypoefficiency-related constraints that have been plaguing you, the exercises you are about to begin will enable you to fulfill yourself and give free rein to your personality. Only when a prisoner has been freed from his ball and chain can he discover that he likes to dance!

That is why this book does not end with the month of training: its final part is devoted to Brain Fitness in life; that is, to various ways of applying it in everyday activities and giving yourself the best chance of putting the odds in your favor.

You will be preparing yourself to play an extraordinary game, against others and especially against yourself. What is at stake? A better way of perceiving people and things and feeling at home in the world. It can be called happiness.

FIRST WEEK

SESSION 1

EXERCISE YOUR PERCEPTIVE ABILITY

A. There is an animal hidden in this drawing. Try to find it in less than **30 seconds**.

Answer:

There is a bird in the mountains to the right of the skaters.

Scoring:

Right answer in less than 30 seconds	2
Right answer in less than 45 seconds	1
Right answer in 45 seconds or more	0

B. Observe these coins for **10 seconds**, then try very quickly, in less than **20 seconds**, to give the total number of coins, the number of different values, and the value that appears only once.

Answer:

Fifteen coins, four different values, the 100-franc coin appears only once.

Scoring:

3 right answers in less than 20 seconds	3
2 right answers in less than 20 seconds	2
2 or 3 right answers in less than 30 seconds	1
Any number of right answers in 30 seconds or more	0

Total score for your perceptive ability (Exercise A + Exercise B) ——

EXERCISE YOUR LOGICAL THINKING

A. Observe this series of letters for **30 seconds**, then try, in less than **45 seconds**, to find the logical way in which the missing letters have been removed.

A B D E F I J K L P Q R S T Y Z A B C D J K L M N O P

Answer:

Two letters (A, B) are left and one (C) is removed; and three (D, E, F) are left and two (G, H) are removed; and so on.

Scoring:

Right answer in less than 45 seconds	2
Right answer in less than 1 minute	1
Right answer in 1 minute or more	0

B. Look at this logical sequence of figures for **30 seconds**, then try to fill in the empty boxes in less than **15 seconds**.

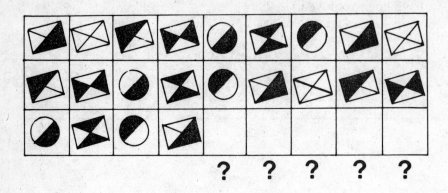

? ? ? ? ?

Answer:

the sequence.
boxes simply continue the order established at the beginning of
The first seven figures are repeated indefinitely, so the last five

Scoring:

Right answer in less than 15 seconds	3
Right answer in 15 seconds	2
Right answer in less than 30 seconds	1
Right answer in 30 seconds or more	0

Total score for your logical thinking (Exercise A +
Exercise B)   ___

EXERCISE YOUR VERBAL ABILITY

Each line below is a word with its letters scrambled. In less than 3 minutes, without writing them down, try to unscramble the words and find the "intruder," the word that has no connection with the others.

```
WARSPOR

HEDACICEK

CUTONCO

ROTHICS

TANASEPH

RUTELVU

SLARTABOS
```

Answer:

Sparrow, chickadee, coconut, ostrich, pheasant, vulture, albatross—all names of birds, except for coconut, which is therefore the "intruder."

Scoring:

Right answer in less than 3 minutes	5
Right answer in 3 minutes	3
Right answer in less than 5 minutes	2
Right answer in 5 minutes or more	0

Score for your verbal ability ___

EXERCISE YOUR SHORT-TERM MEMORY

Slowly, at the rate of about one number per second, read these two series of numbers three times, then close the book and try to write them down in correct order in less than **45 seconds.**

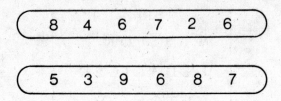

Scoring:

Right answer in less than 45 seconds	5
Right answer in 45 seconds	3
Right answer in less than 1 minute	2
Right answer in 1 minute or more	0

Score for your short-term memory   —

EXERCISE YOUR LONG-TERM MEMORY

Without looking back at the relevant pages, try to answer these questions in less than **45 seconds**:

What are the different values of the coins?

Which one appears only once?

What are the two series of numbers?

Scoring:

3 right answers in less than 45 seconds	10
2 right answers in less than 45 seconds	5
1, 2, or 3 right answers in less than 1 minute	2
Any number of right answers in 1 minute or more	0

Score for your long-term memory ____

You have finished your first session. Now you can take stock of the results.

Score for perceptive ability   ———————

Score for logical thinking   ———————

Score for verbal ability   ———————

Score for short-term memory   ———————

Score for long-term memory   ———————

Add up your scores to get your efficiency rating.

Efficiency rating for the first session
(30 is the highest possible total score):   ———————

SESSION 2

EXERCISE YOUR PERCEPTIVE ABILITY

Observe this array of letters for **10 seconds**.

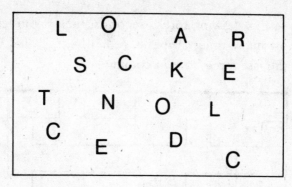

Imagine covering the array with the template below and write in the letters that would appear in the circles. Then, in less than **30 seconds,** find the nine-letter word that can be formed with the letters in the circles.

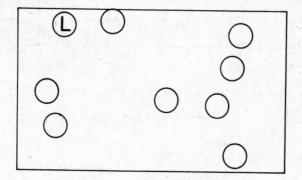

Answer:
The nine-letter word is *collector*.

Scoring:

Right answer in less than 30 seconds	5
Right answer in 30 seconds	3
Right answer in less than 1 minute	1
Right answer in 1 minute or more	0

Score for your perceptive ability ___

EXERCISE YOUR VISUOSPATIAL ABILITY

A. Observe this drawing for **15 seconds**, then say in less than **1 minute** how many times shapes a, b, c, d, e, f, g, and h appear, and what the last three have in common.

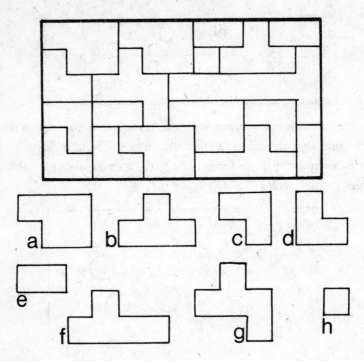

Answer:

common is therefore that they appear only once.
twice; shapes b, f, g, and h, once. What the last three have in
Shapes a and e appear four times; shape d, three times; shape c,

Scoring:

Both right answers in less than 1 minute	3
1 right answer in less than 1 minute	2
Both right answers in 1 minute	2
1 right answer in 1 minute	1
1 or 2 right answers in 1 minute or more	0

B. Observe the solid figure for **15 seconds**. It was obtained by folding one of the flat shapes, 1, 2, or 3. Discover which one in less than **30 seconds**.

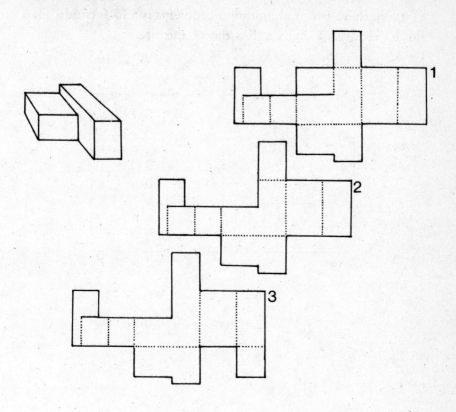

Answer:

The solid figure was obtained by folding flat shape 1.

Scoring:

Right answer in less than 30 seconds	2
Right answer in 30 seconds	1
Right answer in more than 30 seconds	0

Total score for your visuospatial ability (Exercise A + Exercise B) ___

EXERCISE YOUR STRUCTURALIZATION ABILITY

Observe these two multiplication problems for **15 seconds**, then fill in the missing digits in less than **1 minute**.

```
        8 · 3              5 2 ·
      ×   1 ·            ×   4 · 3
      ─────────          ─────────
      1 · 2 ·            1 5 7 ·
        · · 3            2 · 0 ·
      ─────────          2 · · 4
        · · 5 ·          ─────────
                         · 3 3 0 1 ·
```

Answer:

The first multiplication problem is 813 multiplied by 12; the second is 526 times 443.

Scoring:

Both right answers in less than 1 minute	5
1 right answer in less than 1 minute	4
Both right answers in 1 minute	3
1 right answer in 1 minute	1
1 or 2 right answers in more than 1 minute	0

Score for your structuralization ability   ——

EXERCISE YOUR SHORT-TERM MEMORY

Observe these letters for 15 **seconds**, then close the book and time yourself to see how long it takes you to write the word that can be formed using all the letters.

Answer:

The word is formulation.

Scoring:

Right answer in less than 5 seconds	5
Right answer in less than 10 seconds	4
Right answer in less than 15 seconds	2
Right answer in 15 seconds	1
Right answer in more than 15 seconds	0

Score for your short-term memory   ___

EXERCISE YOUR LONG-TERM MEMORY

Without looking back at the relevant pages, try to answer these questions in less than **45 seconds**:

What word could be formed with the letters appearing in the circles in the template?

How many times did shape b appear in the drawing?

What were the missing digits in the multiplication problems?

Scoring:

3 right answers in less than 45 seconds	10
2 right answers in less than 45 seconds	5
1 right answer in less than 45 seconds	3
2 or 3 right answers in less than 1 minute	2
Any number of right answers in 1 minute or more	0

Score for your long-term memory   ____

You have finished your second session. Now you can take stock of the results.

Score for perceptive ability   _____

Score for visuospatial ability   _____

Score for structuralization ability   _____

Score for short-term memory   _____

Score for long-term memory   _____

Add up your scores to get your efficiency rating.

Efficiency rating for the second session: _____

SESSION 3

EXERCISE YOUR VISUOSPATIAL ABILITY

Observe these pencils for **10 seconds**; then, in less than **30 seconds**, find how many different lengths there are, and how many pencils there are of each length.

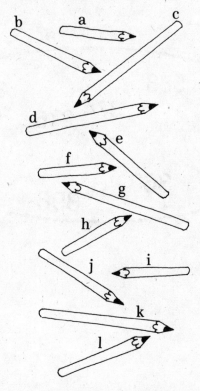

Answer:

There are three different lengths, and four pencils of each length: a, f, h, and i; b, e, j, and l; c, d, g, and k.

Scoring:

Right answer in less than 30 seconds	5
Right answer in 30 seconds	3
Right answer in less than 45 seconds	1
Right answer in 45 seconds or more	0

Score for your visuospatial ability   ___

EXERCISE YOUR STRUCTURALIZATION
ABILITY

A. All but one of these three-digit numbers share a common feature. Observe them for **15 seconds**, then try to find the "intruder" in less than **15 seconds**.

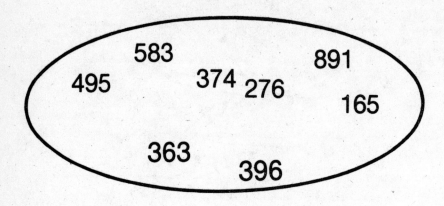

Answer:

In all the numbers except 276, the middle digit is the sum of the other two. Alternate answer: except for 276, the numbers are all composed of one even digit and two odd ones.

Scoring:

Right answer in less than 15 seconds	3
Right answer in 15 seconds	2
Right answer in less than 45 seconds	1
Right answer in 45 seconds or more	0

B. Observe this pyramid of glasses for **10 seconds**; then, in less than **30 seconds**, find the glass that must be taken out to make the pyramid collapse.

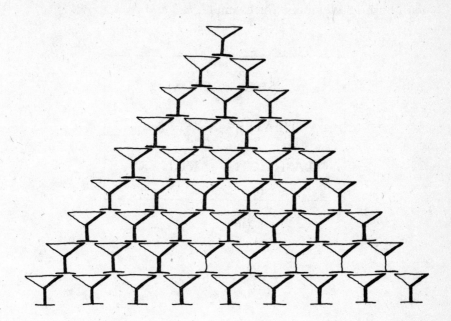

Answer:

The middle (fifth) glass in the bottom row must be taken out to make the pyramid collapse.

Scoring:

Right answer in less than 30 seconds	2
Right answer in 30 seconds	1
Right answer in more than 30 seconds	0

Total score for your structuralization ability (Exercise A + Exercise B) ____

EXERCISE YOUR VERBAL ABILITY

A. Observe these three pairs of words for **15 seconds**; then, in less than **1 minute**, for each pair find a word that can be associated with both its elements (for example, *lock* and *piano: key*).

SHIP—CARDS

THEATER—AIRPLANE

FLASHLIGHT—ARTILLERY

Answer:

For *ship* and *cards: deck;* for *theater* and *airplane: wings;* for *flashlight* and *artillery: battery.*

Scoring:

3 right answers in less than 1 minute	3
2 right answers in less than 1 minute	2
1 right answer in less than 1 minute	1
Any number of right answers in 1 minute or more	0

B. Observe these nine pairs of letters for **15 seconds** and form as many six-letter words as you can with them in less than **2 minutes**. A pair of letters can come at the beginning or end of a word, or in the middle. For example, with *st*: *st*arts, re*st*ed, agha*st*.

```
        EC              SC

VO                           SA
        ID      UC

   LO       HA       EG
```

Answer:

Some of the six-letter words that can be formed are: *scorns, reckon, salted, bucked, afraid, ideals, avowal, lonely, voiced, mellow, halved, begged.*

Scoring:

9 six-letter words in less than 2 minutes	2
9 six-letter words in 2 minutes	1
9 six-letter words in more than 2 minutes	0

Total score for your verbal ability (Exercise A + Exercise B) _____

EXERCISE YOUR SHORT-TERM MEMORY

Observe this map for **3 minutes**; then close the book and, in less than **1 minute**, reproduce the map in as much detail as possible, indicating the street names, public establishments, etc.

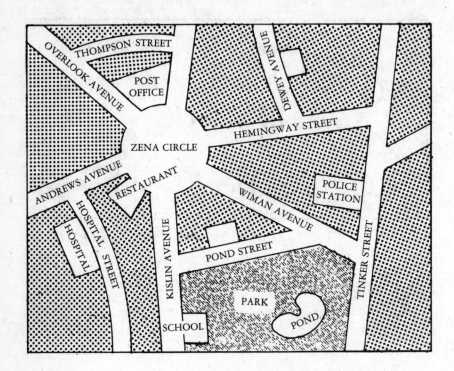

Scoring:

10 or more features of the map in less than 1 minute	5
10 or more features in 1 minute	4
7 to 9 features in less than 1 minute	3
7 to 9 features in 1 minute	2
5 or 6 features in 1 minute	1
Any number of features in more than 1 minute	0

Score for your short-term memory ____

EXERCISE YOUR LONG-TERM MEMORY

Without looking back at the relevant pages, do the following in less than **45 seconds**:

Give the letters of at least one group of pencils of the same length.

Tell which three-digit number was the "intruder."

Give at least five of the nine pairs of letters.

Scoring:

3 right answers in less than 45 seconds	10
2 right answers in less than 45 seconds	5
1 right answer in less than 45 seconds	3
2 or 3 right answers in less than 1 minute	2
Any number of right answers in more than 1 minute	0

Score for your long-term memory _____

You have finished your third session. Now you can take stock of
the results.

Score for visuospatial ability   _____

Score for structuralization ability   _____

Score for verbal ability   _____

Score for short-term memory   _____

Score for long-term memory   _____

Add up your scores to get your efficiency rating.

Efficiency rating for the third session: _____

MAKE A GRAPH OF YOUR PROGRESS IN THE FIRST WEEK

Efficiency rating

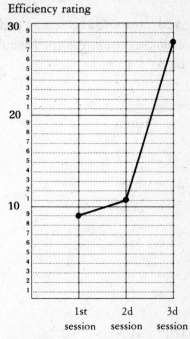

Example of a typical group

In the graph form below the example, mark your efficiency rating for each session with a dot, then connect the three dots with a line. (In the example, I have shown a score of 9 out of 30 for the first session, 11 out of 30 for the second, and 28 out of 30 for the third.)

Efficiency rating

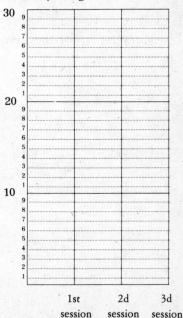

Draw your graph

CALCULATE YOUR EFFICIENCY RATING FOR THE FIRST WEEK

Add up the three scores and divide the total by three. (In the example given, the total would be 9 + 11 + 28 = 48, divided by 3 = 16.)

1st session   _____

2d session   _____

3d session   _____

Total   _____

Divide by three

Efficiency rating for the first week   _____

SECOND WEEK

SECOND WEEK

SESSION 1

EXERCISE YOUR PERCEPTIVE ABILITY

A. Try to find the differences between these two drawings in less than **30 seconds**.

 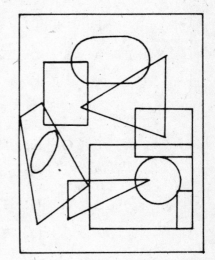

Answer:

There are five differences. In the drawing on the right: the upper-left rectangle is smaller; the right-hand triangle inside the upper-left rectangle is smaller; the upper-middle ellipse does not extend as far into the triangle; the lower-right rectangle does not extend into the circle; the left-hand ellipse is placed differently.

Scoring:

3 right answers in less than 30 seconds	3
2 right answers in less than 30 seconds	2
2 or 3 right answers in 30 seconds	1
Any number of right answers in more than 30 seconds	0

B. Try to discover, in less than **15 seconds**, which word can be formed with the letters at intersections between two words.

```
              W   O   V   E   N

              E

      S   E   A   S   O   N

              S

              E

          A   L   O   N   E

                  O       S

          S   C   U   T   T   L   E

                  N       R

                          E

                      A   S   S   E   R   T

                          S
```

Answer:

The word is *walnuts.*

Scoring:

Right answer in less than 15 seconds	2
Right answer in less than 30 seconds	1
Right answer in 30 seconds or more	0

Total score for your perceptive ability (Exercise A + Exercise B)   ___

EXERCISE YOUR LOGICAL THINKING

A. The clock faces in each of the three rows are arranged in a logical sequence. Try to find the sequence in each row, and draw the missing hands on the three blank faces, in less than **15 seconds**.

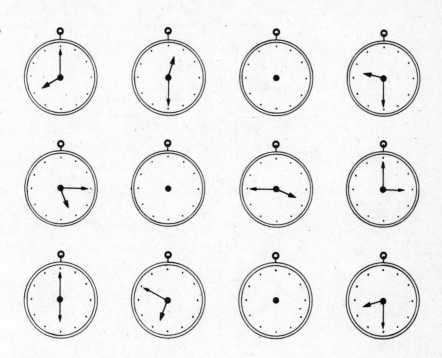

Answer:

The first blank face should show five o'clock (four and a half hours added each time); the second one, four-thirty (forty-five minutes subtracted each time); the third one, seven-forty (fifty minutes added each time).

Scoring:

3 right answers in less than 15 seconds	3
3 right answers in 15 seconds	2
2 or 3 right answers in less than 30 seconds	1
Any number of right answers in 30 seconds or more	0

B. In less than **30 seconds**, give a logical explanation for the top two series of letters, then give the missing letter in each of the bottom two series, following the same principle used in the top two.

B + D = F	R — H = J
C + M = ?	V — ? = G

Answer:

If each letter is replaced with the number of its order in the alphabet ($a = 1$, $b = 2$, $c = 3$, etc.), the two top series are verified: b (2) plus d (4) equals f (6), and r (18) minus h (8) equals j (10). So the two bottom series should be completed as follows: c plus m equals p, and v minus o equals g.

Scoring:

4 right answers in less than 30 seconds	2
3 right answers in less than 30 seconds	1
4 right answers in less than 1 minute	1
Any number of right answers in 1 minute or more	0

Total score for your logical thinking (Exercise A +
Exercise B)   ___

EXERCISE YOUR VERBAL ABILITY

In less than 1 **minute**, add a letter to each of these nine pairs of letters in such a way as to form a three-letter word.

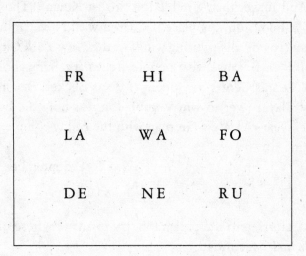

Answer:

For example, one can form: *fry, hip, bat, lap, war, fog, den, net, run.*

Scoring:

9 right answers in less than 1 minute	5
6 to 8 right answers in less than 1 minute	3
6 or more right answers in 1 minute	2
Any number of right answers in more than 1 minute	0

Score for your verbal ability   ___

EXERCISE YOUR SHORT-TERM MEMORY

Read this paragraph slowly, aloud:

Forget that defending U.S. Open champ John McEnroe was nearly eliminated by unseeded Israeli Shlomo Glickstein in the first round. And forget that Wimbledon finalist Kevin ("They should drop an A-bomb on this place") Curren was. Never mind about the rowdy crowds, the swirling winds or the New York City traffic. Forget all that. Because what people are *really* talking about at the National Tennis Center in Queens is Boris Becker. Becoming the youngest player ever to win Wimbledon was only the beginning for the 17-year-old West German with the ruddy complexion and ready grin.

Newsweek, September 9, 1985

Without referring to the paragraph, try to answer these questions in less than **15 seconds**:

What was Boris Becker's age at the time when the article was written?

What other tennis players are mentioned?

Scoring:

2 right answers in less than 15 seconds	5
2 right answers in 15 seconds	3
2 right answers in less than 30 seconds	2
1 or 2 right answers in 30 seconds or more	0

Score for your short-term memory   ____

EXERCISE YOUR LONG-TERM MEMORY

Without looking back at the relevant pages, try to answer these
questions in less than **45 seconds**:

What was the word formed by the letters at intersections between
two words?

What did $c + m$ equal?

What were at least five of the pairs of letters?

Scoring:

    3 right answers in less than 45 seconds   10

    2 right answers in less than 45 seconds   5

    2 or 3 right answers in less than 1 minute   2

    Any number of right answers in 1 minute or more   0

Score for your long-term memory   ____

You have finished your first session. Now you can take stock of the results.

Score for perceptive ability   _____

Score for logical thinking   _____

Score for verbal ability   _____

Score for short-term memory   _____

Score for long-term memory   _____

Add up your scores to get your efficiency rating.

Efficiency rating for the first session   _____

SESSION 2

EXERCISE YOUR PERCEPTIVE ABILITY

Observe this dress for **10 seconds.**

In less than **15 seconds,** say how many different kinds of stripes it has, and how they are arranged.

Answer:

symmetrically above and below the solid black band at the waist.
The dress has five different kinds of stripes, and they are repeated

Scoring:

2 right answers in less than 15 seconds	5
2 right answers in 15 seconds	3
1 or 2 right answers in less than 30 seconds	1
1 or 2 right answers in 30 seconds or more	0

Score for your perceptive ability   ____

EXERCISE YOUR VISUOSPATIAL ABILITY

A. Each of the four lettered shapes (a, e, f, h) fits together with one of the four numbered shapes (1, 2, 3, 4). Observe the shapes for **15 seconds**, then try to group them into four matching pairs in less than **30 seconds**.

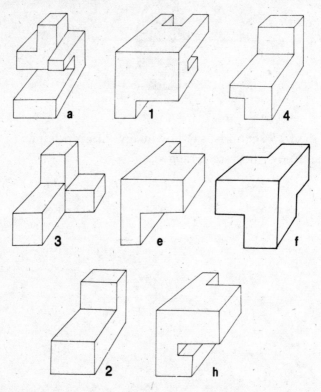

Answer:

a with 1, e with 2, f with 3, h with 4.

Scoring:

4 right answers in less than 30 seconds	3
4 right answers in 30 seconds	2
2 or 3 right answers in less than 30 seconds	2
1 right answer in less than 30 seconds	1
2, 3, or 4 right answers in less than 1 minute	1
Any number of right answers in 1 minute or more	0

B. Observe this three-dimensional figure for **10 seconds**.

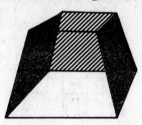

Below, the three-dimensional figure has been "unfolded" to form a two-dimensional figure. In less than **30 seconds**, tell which segments are black, which are diagonally striped, and which are transparent.

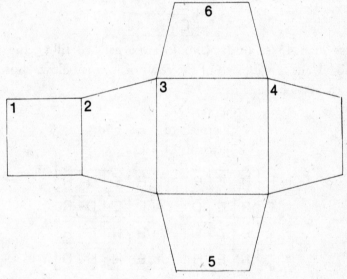

Answer:

One, three and five are transparent, two and four are black, six is diagonally striped.

Scoring:

Right answer in less than 30 seconds	2
Right answer in 30 seconds	1
Right answer in more than 30 seconds	0

Total score for your visuospatial ability (Exercise A + Exercise B)   ___

EXERCISE YOUR STRUCTURALIZATION ABILITY

Look at this grid attentively for 15 seconds.

D	R	D	E
R	D	E	E
		D		1
E	R	D	D
E	D	R	D
				2
R	D	E	D
D	E	R	E

In less than 45 seconds, complete the grid by filling the rows marked 1 and 2 with two of the rows of letters below, chosen in such a way as to obtain:

>   1 diagonal of 4 R's,
>   2 diagonals of 4 E's, and
>   3 diagonals of 4 D's.

b | E | D | E | R   f | R | E | D | R

a | E | R | E | D   e | D | E | D | R

c | R | E | D | D   g | D | R | E | R

d | D | R | E | R   h | E | R | E | D

Answer:

Row 1 must be filled with c, and row 2 with e.

Scoring:

2 right answers in less than 45 seconds	5
1 right answer in less than 45 seconds	4
2 right answers in 45 seconds	3
1 right answer in 45 seconds	1
1 or 2 right answers in more than 45 seconds	0

Score for your structuralization ability   _____

EXERCISE YOUR SHORT-TERM MEMORY

Observe this map of the United States for **45 seconds**; then close the book and, starting at the upper right, try to name the cities included in the itinerary marked out on the map in less than **1 minute**.

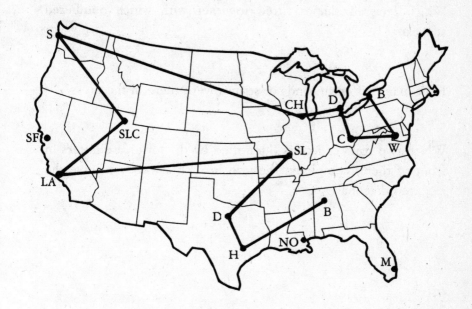

Answer:

Left out: SF: San Francisco; NO: New Orleans; M: Miami.

Birmingham.

Seattle, Salt Lake City, Los Angeles, Saint Louis, Dallas, Houston,

The cities are: Buffalo, Washington, Cincinnati, Detroit, Chicago,

Scoring:

Right answer in less than 1 minute	5
Right answer in less than 30 seconds	4
Right answer in 1 minute 30 seconds	2
Right answer in 2 minutes	1
Right answer in more than 2 minutes	0

Score for your short-term memory   ___

EXERCISE YOUR LONG-TERM MEMORY

Without looking back at the relevant pages, try to answer these questions in less than 45 seconds:

Which lettered shapes fitted together with which numbered shapes?

How many different kinds of stripes were there in the dress?

Which two rows of letters (identified by the lowercase letters in front of them) completed the grid in such a way as to give the required diagonals?

Scoring:

    3 right answers in less than 45 seconds   10

    2 right answers in less than 45 seconds   5

    1 right answer in less than 45 seconds   3

    2 or 3 right answers in less than 1 minute   2

    Any number of right answers in 1 minute or more   0

Score for your long-term memory   ____

You have finished your second session. Now you can take stock of the results.

Score for perceptive ability   _____

Score for visuospatial ability   _____

Score for structuralization ability   _____

Score for short-term memory   _____

Score for long-term memory   _____

Add up your scores to get your efficiency rating.

Efficiency rating for the second session: _____

SESSION 3

EXERCISE YOUR VISUOSPATIAL ABILITY

Observe this map for **45 seconds**, using the coordinates (numbers and letters); then try, in less than **45 seconds**, to give the coordinates (for example, h 5, g–h 3) of the church, the bank, the school, the city hall, the grocery store, the park, and the subway entrance.

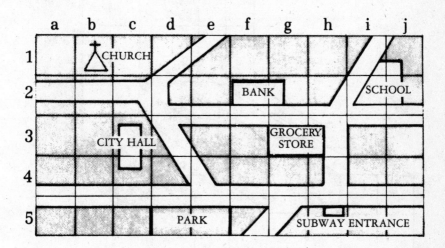

Answer:

The church is at b 1, the bank at f–g 2, the school at i–j 1–2, the city hall at c 3–4, the grocery store at g–h 3, the park at d–e 5, the subway entrance at h 5.

Scoring:

5 or more right answers in less than 45 seconds	5
4 right answers in less than 45 seconds	2
3 right answers in less than 45 seconds	1
Any number of right answers in 45 seconds or more	0

Total for your visuospatial ability ___

EXERCISE YOUR STRUCTURALIZATION ABILITY

A. Observe this pile of blocks for **10 seconds**; then try to determine, in less than **30 seconds**, how many more blocks are needed to fill the pile up solid to its highest level.

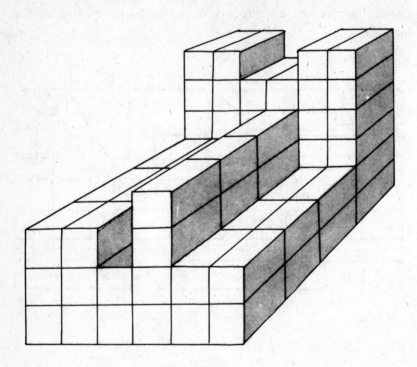

Answer:
Sixty-two are needed.

Scoring:
Right answer in less than 30 seconds	2
Right answer in 30 seconds	1
Right answer in more than 30 seconds	0

B. Observe these letters for **30 seconds**; then try, in less than **30 seconds**, to form at least five words containing the combination *ain* and two or more of the single letters: for example, *taints, slain.*

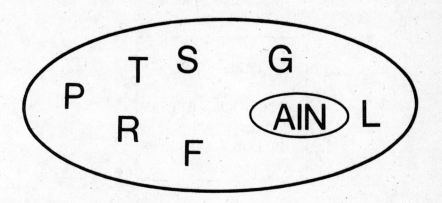

Answer:

Other examples: paint, rains, stain, plain, sprain, grain.

Scoring:

5 or more words in less than 30 seconds	3
5 or more words in 30 seconds	2
5 or more words in 45 seconds	1
Any number of words in more than 45 seconds	0

Total score for your structuralization ability (Exercise A + Exercise B)   ___

EXERCISE YOUR VERBAL ABILITY

A. Observe these pairs of words for **10 seconds**; then, in less than **45 seconds**, find a word for each pair that can be associated with both its elements (for example, *lock* and *piano*: *key*).

> TREE—CAR
>
> SCHOOL—EYE
>
> PILLOW—COURT

Answer:

case.

For tree and car: trunk; for school and eye: pupil; for pillow and court:

Scoring:

2 or 3 right answers in less than 45 seconds	2
Any number of right answers in 45 seconds	1
Any number of right answers in more than 45 seconds	0

B. Observe these letters for **30 seconds**; then try, in less than **45 seconds,** to replace the question marks with letters in such a way as to form at least six words ending in *al* (for example, F? U?: *FEUDAL*).

<table>
<tr><td>L ? C</td><td rowspan="8"></td></tr>
<tr><td>N? R?</td></tr>
<tr><td>T ? T</td></tr>
<tr><td>E ? U</td></tr>
<tr><td>R ? G</td></tr>
<tr><td>S ? G?</td></tr>
<tr><td>I ? E</td></tr>
<tr><td>R ? S ?</td></tr>
</table>

AL

Answer:

Local, normal, total, equal, regal, signal, ideal, rascal.

Scoring:

6 or more words in 45 seconds	3
4 or 5 words in 45 seconds	2
6 or more words in 1 minute	1
Any number of words in more than 1 minute	0

Total score for your verbal ability (Exercise A + Exercise B)   ___

EXERCISE YOUR SHORT-TERM MEMORY

Observe these objects for **30 seconds**; then close the book and try to recall at least ten of them, not necessarily in order, in less than **1 minute**.

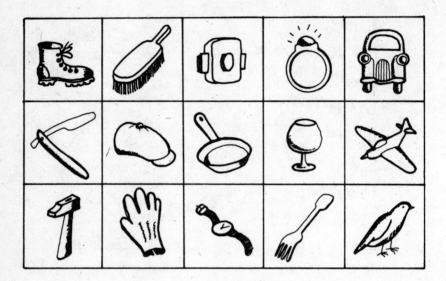

Scoring:

10 or more objects in less than 1 minute	5
10 or more objects in 1 minute	4
7 to 9 objects in less than 1 minute	3
7 to 9 objects in 1 minute	2
5 or 6 objects in 1 minute	1
Any number of objects in more than 1 minute	0

Score for your short-term memory   ___

EXERCISE YOUR LONG-TERM MEMORY

Without looking back at the relevant pages, try to answer these questions in less than **45 seconds**:

What were the coordinates (numbers and letters) of the city hall, the school, and the grocery store?

How many blocks were needed to fill the pile?

What were at least five of the words ending in *al*?

Scoring:

3 right answers in less than 45 seconds	10
2 right answers in less than 45 seconds	5
1 right answer in less than 45 seconds	3
2 or 3 right answers in less than 1 minute	2
Any number of right answers in 1 minute or more	0

Score for your long-term memory   ___

You have finished your third session. Now you can take stock of
the results.

Score for visuospatial ability   _____

Score for structuralization ability   _____

Score for verbal ability   _____

Score for short-term memory   _____

Score for long-term memory   _____

Add up your scores to get your efficiency rating.

Efficiency rating for the third session: _____

MAKE A GRAPH OF YOUR PROGRESS IN THE SECOND WEEK

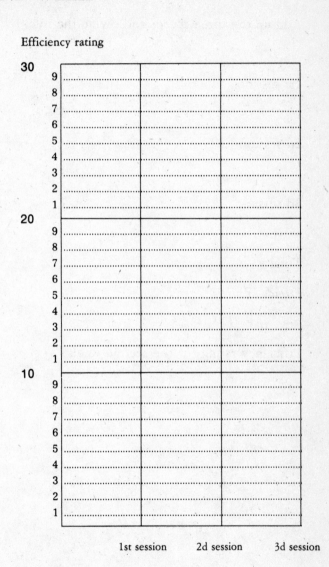

If you have any difficulties, refer to page 103

CALCULATE YOUR EFFICIENCY RATING FOR THE SECOND WEEK

Add up the three scores and divide the total by three.

1st session   ———

2d session   ———

3d session   ———

Total   ———

Divide by three

Efficiency rating for the second week   ———

THIRD WEEK

SESSION 1

EXERCISE YOUR PERCEPTIVE ABILITY

A. Observe these glasses for **10 seconds**; then, in less than **15 seconds**, determine how many you see.

Answer:

There are twenty glasses.

Scoring:

Right answer in less than 15 seconds	2
Right answer in 15 seconds	1
Right answer in more than 15 seconds	0

B. Observe this drawing for 30 seconds.

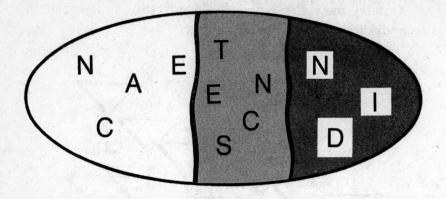

In less than **45 seconds**, give the four words that can be formed as follows: one with the letters in the white section, one with those in the light gray section, one with those in the dark gray section, and one with those in all three sections taken together.

Answer:

In the white section: *cane;* in the light gray section: *scent* or *cents;* in the dark gray section: *din;* in all three sections: *incandescent.*

Scoring:

4 right answers in less than 45 seconds	3
2 or 3 right answers in less than 45 seconds	2
3 or 4 right answers in 1 minute	1
Fewer than 3 right answers in 1 minute	0

Score for your perceptive ability   ____

EXERCISE YOUR LOGICAL THINKING

A. Observe this pyramid for **15 seconds**; then try, in less than **45 seconds**, to fill in the numbered squares with the appropriate designs (vertical lines, horizontal lines, solid, dots) in accordance with the logical sequence of designs.

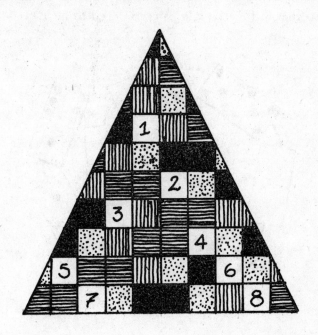

Answer:

solid, eight; horizontal lines.

one and three, dots; two, four, five, and seven, vertical lines; six,

right to left; then the same from left to right; and so on. Therefore:

First: solid, dots, vertical lines, horizontal lines; then the same from

Scoring:

At least 6 right answers in less than 45 seconds	2
At least 4 right answers in 45 seconds	1
Any number of right answers in more than 45 seconds	0

B. This logical sequence of dominoes starts at the outside of the spiral and goes inward. Observe it for **20 seconds**, then try to fill in the dots on the blank dominoes in less than **2 minutes**, using the principle of the sequence. (Note: since 6 is the maximum number of dots on either half of a domino, if the sequence yields a number larger than 6 it is treated as if it went up to 6 and "started over," so that 7, for example, is considered to be 1.)

Answer:

fore 2–5, 4–3, and 2–5.

two on the right. The numbers for the blank dominoes are there-

The sequence is obtained by always adding one on the left and

Scoring:

3 right answers in less than 2 minutes	3
1 or 2 right answers in less than 2 minutes	2
1, 2, or 3 right answers in 2 minutes	1
1, 2, or 3 right answers in more than 2 minutes	0

Total score for your logical thinking (Exercise A +
Exercise B)   ___

EXERCISE YOUR VERBAL ABILITY

Observe this grid for **30 seconds**; then, in less than **3 minutes**, fill in the empty squares to form four words.

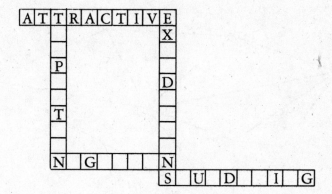

Answer:

Temptation, negation, expeditions, shuddering.

Scoring:

4 right answers in less than 3 minutes	5
4 right answers in 3 minutes	3
4 right answers in less than 5 minutes	2
4 right answers in 5 minutes or more	0

Score for your verbal ability _____

EXERCISE YOUR SHORT-TERM MEMORY

Observe this figure for **15 seconds**, then close the book and try to draw it in less than **1 minute**.

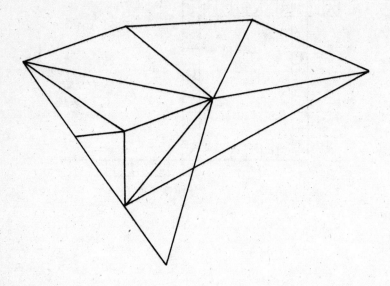

Scoring:

    Right answer in less than 1 minute   5

    Right answer in 1 minute   3

    Right answer in less than 2 minutes   2

    Right answer in 2 minutes or more   0

Score for your short-term memory   ————

EXERCISE YOUR LONG-TERM MEMORY

Without looking back at the relevant pages, try to answer these questions in less than **45 seconds**:

How many glasses were there?

What four words were formed when the empty squares were filled in?

What were the three missing dominoes?

Scoring:

3 right answers in less than 45 seconds	10
2 right answers in less than 45 seconds	5
1 right answer in less than 45 seconds	3
2 or 3 right answers in less than 1 minute	2
Any number of right answers in 1 minute or more	0

Score for your long-term memory   ____

You have finished your first session. Now you can take stock of the results.

Score for perceptive ability   _____

Score for logical thinking   _____

Score for verbal ability   _____

Score for short-term memory   _____

Score for long-term memory   _____
Add up your scores to get your efficiency rating.

Efficiency rating for the first session: _____

SESSION 2

EXERCISE YOUR PERCEPTIVE ABILITY

A. Observe these books for **15 seconds**; then, in less than **20 seconds**, determine how many there are.

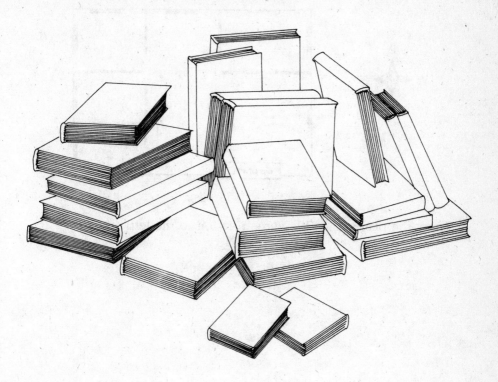

Answer:

There are 21 books.

Scoring:

    Right answer in less than 20 seconds   2

    Right answer in less than 30 seconds   1

    Right answer in 30 seconds or more   0

B. Observe this plan for **15 seconds**, imagining it rotated 90 degrees to the left, then try to draw it in that position, below, in less than **15 seconds**.

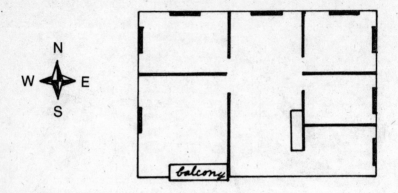

Draw the plan with a 90-degree rotation to the left:

Answer:

If the plan is correctly drawn with a 90-degree rotation to the left, the balcony will be on the right.

Scoring:

Right answer in less than 15 seconds	3
Right answer in less than 45 seconds	2
Right answer in 45 seconds	1
Right answer in more than 45 seconds	0

Total score for your perceptive ability (Exercise A + Exercise B)   ___

EXERCISE YOUR VISUOSPATIAL ABILITY

Observe this drawing for **30 seconds,** then try to determine in less than **1 minute** how many times each of the four shapes inside it (a, b, c, and d) appears.

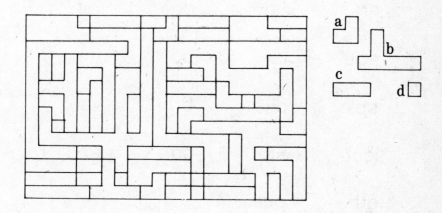

Answer:

Shape a: eight times; shape b: two; shape c: five; shape d: seven.

Scoring:

Right answer in less than 1 minute	5
Right answer in 1 minute	3
Right answer in less than 2 minutes	1
Right answer in 2 minutes or more	0

Score for your visuospatial ability   ___

EXERCISE YOUR STRUCTURALIZATION ABILITY

Here are seven "chopped-up" words. Observe them for 30 seconds, then try to put them back together in less than 2 minutes.

en	tal	dge	ref
nou	ue	ho	mp
spi	ose	bri	val
lect	str	co	an
gth	nce		

Answer:

compose.

The words are: announce, strength, reflect, value, hospital, bridge,

Scoring:

6 or 7 right answers in less than 2 minutes	5
6 or 7 right answers in less than 3 minutes	3
4 or 5 right answers in less than 3 minutes	2
Any number of right answers in 3 minutes or more	0

Score for your structuralization ability   ___

EXERCISE YOUR SHORT-TERM MEMORY

Observe this grid for **15 seconds**, then close the book and try to reproduce it as quickly as you can.

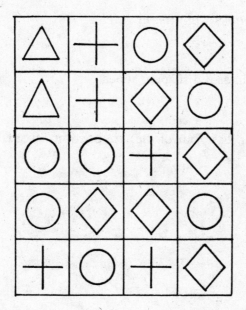

Scoring:

Right answer in less than 15 seconds	5
Right answer in 15 seconds	4
Right answer in less than 45 seconds	2
Right answer in 45 seconds	1
Right answer in more than 45 seconds	0

Score for your short-term memory   ___

EXERCISE YOUR LONG-TERM MEMORY

Without looking back at the relevant pages, try to answer these questions in less than 30 **seconds**:

How many books were there?

How many times did shape c appear?

What were at least four of the "chopped-up" words?

Scoring:

3 right answers in less than 30 seconds	10
2 right answers in less than 30 seconds	5
1 right answer in less than 30 seconds	3
2 or 3 right answers in less than 1 minute	2
Any number of right answers in 1 minute or more	0

Score for your long-term memory   ——

You have finished your second session. Now you can take stock of the results.

Score for perceptive ability   _____

Score for visuospatial ability   _____

Score for structuralization ability   _____

Score for short-term memory   _____

Score for long-term memory   _____

Add up your scores to get your efficiency rating.

Efficiency rating for the second session: _____

SESSION 3

EXERCISE YOUR VISUOSPATIAL ABILITY

Observe this drawing for **15 seconds**, then try to answer the following three questions in less than **30 seconds**. How many socks are there? Which are more numerous, the long ones or the short ones? How many have the same design?

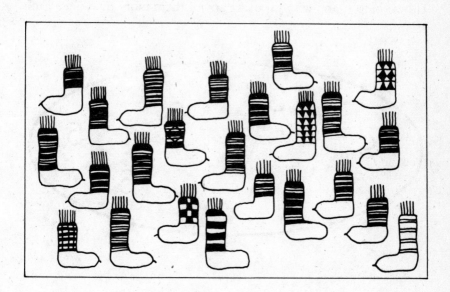

Answer:

white stripes separated by a black one.
socks (four short and one long) have the same design; pairs of
Five. 14. socks 24 are There numerous. more are ones short The

Scoring:

3 right answers in less than 30 seconds	5
3 right answers in 30 seconds	3
3 right answers in less than 45 seconds	1
3 right answers in 45 seconds or more	0

Score for your visuospatial ability ___

EXERCISE YOUR STRUCTURALIZATION ABILITY

A. Observe these numbers for **15 seconds**, then try to do the following in less than **1 minute**: find the sum of the numbers and obtain that sum at least four times by multiplication or a combination of addition and multiplication, using only the numbers shown below, and without using any of them more than once each time.

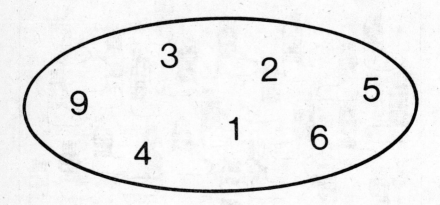

Answer:

and so on.

The sum of the numbers is 30: 6 times 2, plus 5, 3, 9, and 1 equals 30; 6 times 5 equals 30; 3 times 6, plus 5, 4, 2, and 1 equals 30;

Scoring:

At least 4 right answers in less than 1 minute	3
At least 4 right answers in 1 minute	2
At least 4 right answers in less than 2 minutes	1
Any number of right answers in 2 minutes or more	0

B. Observe this picture for **30 seconds**, then try in less than **45 seconds** to find in which empty squares (1, 2, 3, 4, 5) the detached pieces (A, B, C, D, E) fit.

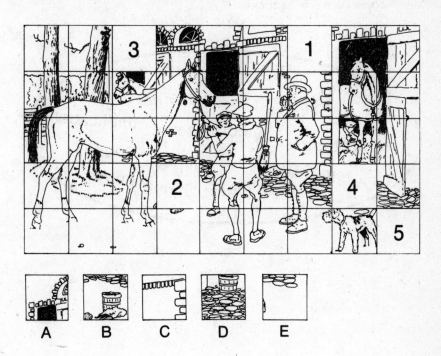

Answer:

C: 1; B: 2; A: 3; D: 4; E: 5

Scoring:

Right answer in less than 45 seconds	2
Right answer in 30 seconds	1
Right answer in more than 30 seconds	0

Total score for your structuralization ability (Exercise A + Exercise B) ___

EXERCISE YOUR VERBAL ABILITY

A. Observe these words for **30 seconds**; then try, in less than **45 seconds**, to find which three of them contain the same group of three consecutive consonants.

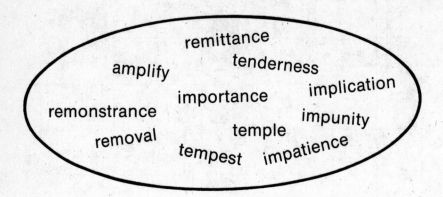

Answer:

The group of consonants is *mpl*, and the words containing it are *temple, amplify,* and *implication.*

Scoring:

3 right answers in less than 45 seconds	3
3 right answers in 45 seconds	2
3 right answers in less than 1 minute	1
Any number of right answers in 1 minute or more	0

B. Observe these letters for **15 seconds**; then try to find, in less than **30 seconds**, the word that can be formed with the unenclosed letters and those enclosed in circles, and the word that can be formed with the unenclosed letters and those enclosed in squares.

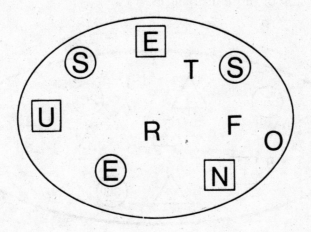

Answer:

squares: *fortune.*

With the letters enclosed in circles: *forests;* with those enclosed in

Scoring:

2 right answers in less than 30 seconds	2
2 right answers in 30 seconds	1
1 or 2 right answers in more than 30 seconds	0

Total score for your verbal ability (Exercise A + Exercise B)   ____

EXERCISE YOUR SHORT-TERM MEMORY

Observe these numbers for **30 seconds**; then close the book and try, in less than **30 seconds**, to remember how many numbers are in circles, how many are in squares, how many are in triangles, and the sum of those in triangles.

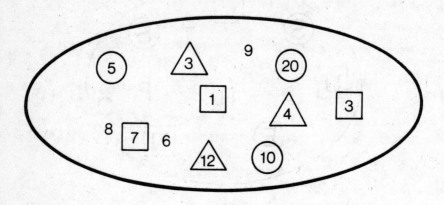

Answer:

There are three numbers in circles, three in squares, and three in triangles. The sum of the numbers in triangles is 19.

Scoring:

    3 right answers in less than 30 seconds   5

    3 right answers in 30 seconds   4

    3 right answers in less than 45 seconds   3

    3 right answers in 45 seconds   2

    3 right answers in less than 1 minute   1

    Any number of right answers in 1 minute or more   0

Score for your short-term memory   _____

EXERCISE YOUR LONG-TERM MEMORY

Without looking back at the relevant pages, try to remember, in less than 30 **seconds**:

The total number of socks

The three words containing *mpl*

The sum of all the numbers in the last exercise

Scoring:

    3 right answers in less than 30 seconds   10

    2 right answers in less than 30 seconds   5

    1 right answer in less than 30 seconds   3

    2 or 3 right answers in less than 1 minute   2

    Any number of right answers in 1 minute or more   0

Score for your long-term memory   ——

You have finished your third session. Now you can take stock of the results.

Score for visuospatial ability   _____

Score for structuralization ability   _____

Score for verbal ability   _____

Score for short-term memory   _____

Score for long-term memory   _____

Add up your scores to get your efficiency rating.

Efficiency rating for the third session: _____

MAKE A GRAPH OF YOUR PROGRESS IN THE THIRD WEEK

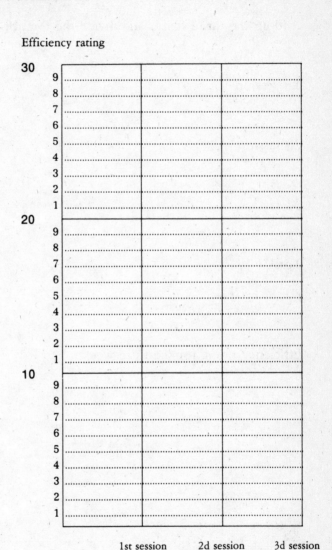

Efficiency rating

If you have difficulties, refer to page 103.

CALCULATE YOUR EFFICIENCY RATING FOR THE THIRD WEEK

Add up the three scores and divide the total by three.

1st session   _____

2d session   _____

3d session   _____

Total   _____

Divide by three

Efficiency rating for the third week   _____

FOURTH WEEK

SESSION 1

EXERCISE YOUR PERCEPTIVE ABILITY

A. Observe these two vases for **20 seconds**, then try to pick out five differences between them in less than **20 seconds**.

Vase 1

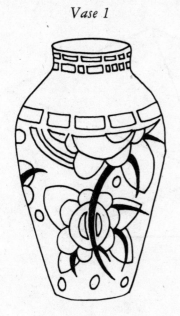

Vase 2

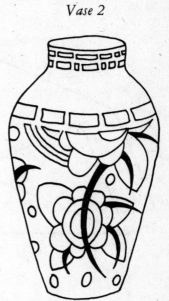

Answer:

has one more oval.

That same flower lacks one black pistil. The left edge of vase 2 lower flower on vase 2 lacks the two oblong shapes at the center. more figures. The upper flower on vase 1 has one more petal. The The second row of decorations on the neck of vase 1 contains

Scoring:

5 right answers in less than 20 seconds	3
3 or 4 right answers in less than 20 seconds	2
2 to 5 right answers in less than 30 seconds	1
Any number of right answers in 30 seconds or more	0

B. Observe this figure for **10 seconds**; then try to determine in less than **20 seconds** how many squares, rectangles, and triangles it contains.

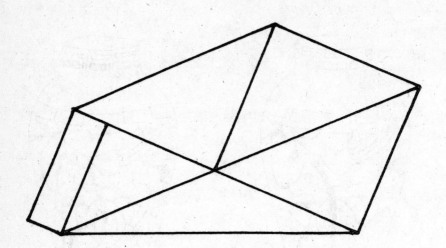

Answer:

One square, one rectangle, seven triangles.

Scoring:

Right answer in less than 20 seconds	2
Right answer in less than 30 seconds	1
Right answer in 30 seconds or more	0

Total score for your perceptive ability (Exercise A + Exercise B)   ___

EXERCISE YOUR VERBAL ABILITY

Look at these words for **30 seconds**; then try, in less than 1 minute, to determine what they have in common, and specify four
categories into which they can be divided.

THIMBLE

HOE

SPADE

SCISSORS

BELLOWS

CHISEL

RAKE

RASP

ANVIL

SAW

DRILL

NEEDLE

Answer:

They are all names of tools and they can be classified according
to the people who use them: blacksmith: anvil, bellows; gardener:
hoe, rake, spade; tailor or dressmaker: needle, thimble, scissors;
carpenter or cabinetmaker: saw, chisel, drill, rasp.

Scoring:

4 right answers in less than 1 minute	5
4 right answers in 1 minute	3
4 right answers in less than 2 minutes	2
Any number of right answers in 2 minutes or more	0

Score for your verbal ability   ___

EXERCISE YOUR LOGICAL THINKING

A. Observe this logical sequence of numbers for **30 seconds**, then try to find the missing number in less than **1 minute**.

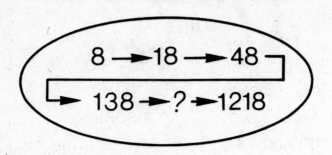

Answer:

equals 138; and so on.

number: 8 plus 10 equals 18; 18 plus 30 equals 48; 48 plus 90

on; that is, continue adding three times as much to each succeeding

first number, 30 to the second one, 90 to the third one, and so

minus 6 equals 48. Another rule is to add 10 to the

3 equals 24, minus 6 equals 18; 18 multiplied by 3 equals 54,

is to multiply each number by 3 and subtract 6: 8 multiplied by

The missing number is 408. One rule for obtaining the sequence

Scoring:

Right answer in less than 1 minute	2
Right answer in 1 minute	1
Right answer in more than 1 minute	0

B. Look at the eight numbered pictures on the next page for 30 seconds. They are not in logical order. Try to find an order for them that will make them tell a story, in less than 30 seconds.

Answer:

The logical order of the pictures can be: eight, six, two, three, five, four, one, seven.

Scoring:

Right answer in less than 30 seconds	3
Right answer in 30 seconds	2
Right answer in less than 1 minute	1
Right answer in 1 minute or more	0

Total score for your logical thinking (Exercise A + Exercise B)   ___

EXERCISE YOUR SHORT-TERM MEMORY

Observe these numbers for **30 seconds**, then close the book and try to remember all the *different* numbers (if a number appears more than once, count it only once) in less than **30 seconds**.

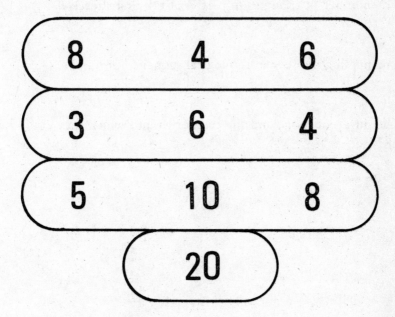

Scoring:

7 right answers in less than 30 seconds	5
4 to 7 right answers in less than 45 seconds	3
4 to 7 right answers in less than 1 minute	2
Any number of right answers in 1 minute or more	0

Score for your short-term memory   ___

EXERCISE YOUR LONG-TERM MEMORY

Without looking back at the relevant pages, try to remember in less than 30 seconds:

The number of triangles in part B of the first exercise.

The missing number in the logical sequence of numbers.

The different tools, and the categories into which they could be divided.

Scoring:

3 right answers in less than 30 seconds	10
2 right answers in less than 30 seconds	5
1 right answer in less than 30 seconds	3
2 or 3 right answers in less than 45 seconds	2
Any number of right answers in 45 seconds or more	0

Score for your long-term memory   ____

You have finished your first session. Now you can take stock of
the results.

Score for perceptive ability   _____

Score for logical thinking   _____

Score for verbal ability   _____

Score for short-term memory   _____

Score for long-term memory   _____
Add up your scores to get your efficiency rating.

Efficiency rating for the first session: _____

SESSION 2

EXERCISE YOUR PERCEPTIVE ABILITY

Observe these bottle caps for **10 seconds**.

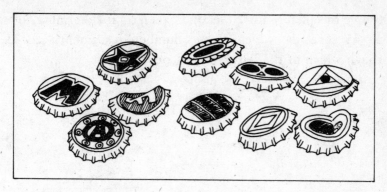

Try to find, in less than **15 seconds**, the cap that is not in the first picture.

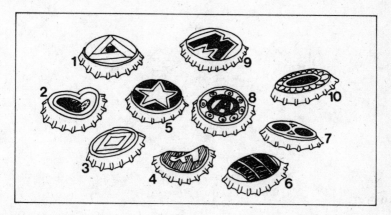

Answer:

The cap numbered 5 is not in the first picture.

Scoring:

Right answer in less than 15 seconds	5
Right answer in 15 seconds	3
Right answer in less than 30 seconds	1
Right answer in 30 seconds or more	0

Score for your perceptive ability _____

EXERCISE YOUR VISUOSPATIAL ABILITY

Observe this picture for **20 seconds**; then try to determine, in less than **45 seconds**, which of the numbered segments are seen through which of the lettered telescopes.

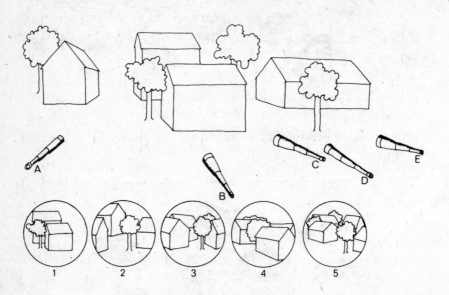

Answer:

2 through d, and 5 through e.

Segment 3 is seen through telescope a, 1 through b, 4 through c,

Scoring:

5 right answers in less than 45 seconds	5
5 right answers in 45 seconds	3
3 or 4 right answers in 45 seconds	2
3 to 5 right answers in less than 1 minute	1
Any number of right answers in 1 minute or more	0

Score for your visuospatial ability   ___

EXERCISE YOUR STRUCTURALIZATION ABILITY

Observe these letters for 30 seconds.

Now try, in less than 45 seconds, to give four words that can be formed as follows: one with the letters in the left-hand section, one with those in the middle section, one with those in the right-hand section, and one with those in all three sections taken together.

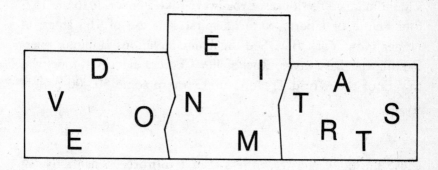

Answer:

onstrative.

In the left-hand section, *dove;* in the middle section, *mine* or *mien;* in the right-hand section, *start* or *tarts;* in all three sections, *dem-*

Scoring:

4 right answers in less than 45 seconds	5
3 right answers in less than 45 seconds	4
4 right answers in 1 minute	3
1 to 3 right answers in 1 minute	1
Any number of right answers in more than 1 minute	0

Score for your structuralization ability   ___

EXERCISE YOUR SHORT-TERM MEMORY

Read this paragraph attentively for **3 minutes**.

Visit New York, one of the most exciting cities in the world. Go to the 1,250-foot Empire State Building; from its observation terraces on the 86th and 102d floors, you'll get a never-to-be-forgotten view. See Fifth Avenue, with its large department stores; the boutiques of Greenwich Village and Soho; elegant restaurants and intimate coffeehouses; Broadway. Take a boat ride to the 152-foot Statue of Liberty, with its spiral staircase of 168 steps, in Upper New York Bay. See the United Nations Building overlooking the East River; Rockefeller Center; the 1,378-foot twin towers of the World Trade Center, where some 50,000 people work.

Close the book and try, in less than **1 minute**, to name five of the places of interest that you are advised to visit in New York City, and give the height of the Empire State Building.

Scoring:

6 right answers in less than 1 minute	5
4 or 5 right answers in less than 1 minute	4
6 right answers in 2 minutes	2
3 to 5 right answers in 2 minutes	1
Any number of right answers in more than 2 minutes	0

Score for your short-term memory   ——

EXERCISE YOUR LONG-TERM MEMORY

Without looking back at the relevant pages, try to answer these questions in less than **30 seconds**:

What was the number of the bottle cap that was not in the first picture?

What four words could be formed with the letters in the different sections?

What were five of the places of interest mentioned in the paragraph on New York City?

Scoring:

3 right answers in less than 30 seconds	10
2 right answers in less than 30 seconds	5
1 right answer in less than 30 seconds	1
2 or 3 right answers in less than 1 minute	2
Any number of right answers in 1 minute or more	0

Score for your long-term memory   ___

You have finished your second session. Now you can take stock of the results.

Score for perceptive ability   _____

Score for visuospatial ability   _____

Score for structuralization ability   _____

Score for short-term memory   _____

Score for long-term memory   _____

Add up your scores to get your efficiency rating.

Efficiency rating for the second session: _____

SESSION 3

EXERCISE YOUR VISUOSPATIAL ABILITY

Observe the plan of this apartment for **30 seconds**.

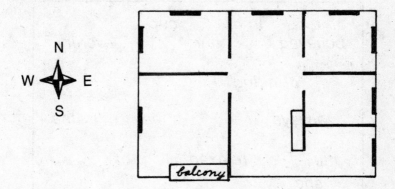

Imagine rotating the plan so that the balcony faces west, then try to draw it in that position, as accurately as possible, in less than **45 seconds**.

Scoring:

Right answer in less than 45 seconds	5
Right answer in 45 seconds	3
Right answer in less than 1 minute	1
Right answer in 1 minute or more	0

Score for your visuospatial ability _____

EXERCISE YOUR STRUCTURALIZATION ABILITY

A. Observe these words for 15 seconds.

in	*cup*	
believed	*her*	*evening*
drinking		
always	*feel*	*tea*
had	*relaxed*	*of*
she		
made	*a*	*more*
the	*that*	

Try to form a sentence with these words in less than 45 seconds.

Answer:

She had always believed that drinking a cup of tea in the evening made her feel more relaxed.

Scoring:

Right answer in less than 45 seconds	3
Right answer in 45 seconds	2
Right answer in less than 1 minute	1
Right answer in 1 minute or more	0

B. Observe this plate for **30 seconds**. Then, in less than **2 minutes**, give the order in which the numbered pieces must be glued together, starting at the center, to reconstruct the plate.

Answer:

The pieces must be glued together in this order: one, three, six, five, two, nine, four, ten, seven, fifteen, eight, eleven, fourteen, thirteen, twelve.

Scoring:

Right answer in less than 2 minutes	2
Right answer in 2 minutes	1
Right answer in more than 2 minutes	0

Total score for your structuralization ability (Exercise A + Exercise B) ___

EXERCISE YOUR VERBAL ABILITY

A. Each of these pairs of letters is the beginning of a word. The words all designate things that are often found in supermarkets. Observe the pairs of letters for **15 seconds**, then try to find the words in less than **2 minutes**.

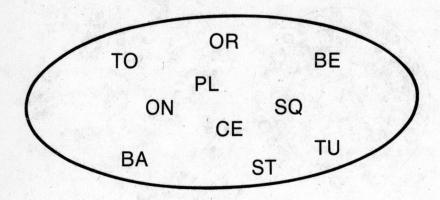

Answer:

Oranges, tomatoes, beans, plums, onions, squash, celery, bananas, turnips, strawberries.

Scoring:

10 right answers in less than 2 minutes	3
7 to 9 right answers in less than 2 minutes	2
4 to 6 right answers in less than 2 minutes	1
Any number of right answers in 2 minutes or more	0

B. The word *winter*, for example, has associations that may suggest other words to you, such as *cold, coat, snow, ski,* and so on. Try to think of at least five words associated with each of the following, in less than **45 seconds:**

```
┌─────────────────────────────────────────────────┐
│                                                  │
│   RIVER: _____        │
│   _____       │
│   _____       │
│                                                  │
│   HORSE: _____        │
│   _____       │
│   _____       │
│                                                  │
│   TREE: _____        │
│   _____       │
│   _____       │
│                                                  │
└─────────────────────────────────────────────────┘
```

Answer:

Some examples of associated words: for *river: bank, water, current, flood, bridge, boat;* for *horse: cowboy, riding, buggy, saddle, jockey, racing;* for *tree: forest, shade, Christmas, leaves, wood, climbing.*

Scoring:

5 associations for each word in less than 45 seconds   2

5 associations for each word in 45 seconds   1

Any number of associations in more than 45 seconds   0

Total score for your verbal ability (Exercise A + Exercise B)   ___

EXERCISE YOUR SHORT-TERM MEMORY

Observe these two groups of letters for **30 seconds**; then close the book and, in less than **45 seconds**, try to find the word that can be formed with the letters in each group.

```
T A F N O F E T A I C E
```

```
H E R N D I L C
```

Answer:

The first word is *affectionate*, the second is *children*.

Scoring:

2 right answers in less than 45 seconds	5
2 right answers in 45 seconds	4
2 right answers in less than 1 minute	3
2 right answers in 1 minute	2
1 right answer in less than 1 minute	1
1 right answer in 1 minute	0

Score for your short-term memory   ——

EXERCISE YOUR LONG-TERM MEMORY

Without looking back at the relevant pages, try to do the following in less than **30 seconds**:

Give the number of pieces into which the plate was broken.

Give at least eight of the words in the two exercises of verbal ability.

Give the words that could be formed with the two groups of letters.

Scoring:

3 right answers in less than 30 seconds	10
2 right answers in less than 30 seconds	5
2 or 3 right answers in less than 1 minute	2
Any number of right answers in 1 minute or more	0

Score for your long-term memory   ____

You have finished your third session. Now you can take stock of the results.

Score for visuospatial ability   _____

Score for structuralization ability   _____

Score for verbal ability   _____

Score for short-term memory   _____

Score for long-term memory   _____
Add up your scores to get your efficiency rating.

Efficiency rating for the third session: _____

MAKE A GRAPH OF YOUR PROGRESS IN THE FOURTH WEEK

Efficiency rating

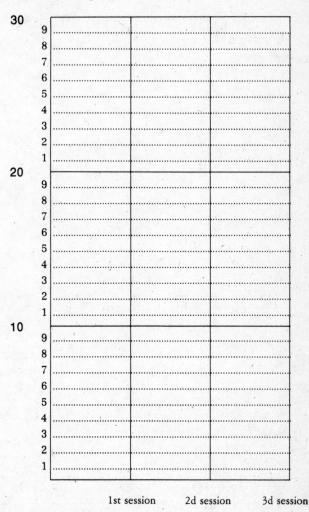

If you have any difficulties, refer to page 103.

CALCULATE YOUR EFFICIENCY RATING FOR THE FOURTH WEEK

Add up the three scores and divide the total by three.

1st session   _____

2d session   _____

3d session   _____

Total   _____

Divide by three

Efficiency rating for the fourth week   _____

MAKE A GRAPH OF YOUR PROGRESS IN THE MONTH

Indicate your efficiency rating for each of the four weeks (refer to pages 104, 131, 160, and 188), and draw the graph by connecting the four dots with a line.

Efficiency rating

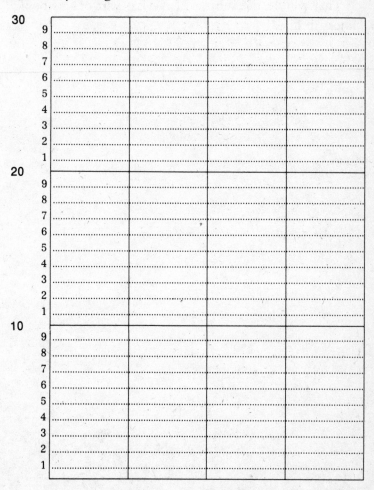

1st week   2d week   3d week   4th week

Now you can draw conclusions from those figures.

Even if your scores are modest, but have improved from one session to the next, and then from one week to the next, that fact is very positive. If the trend is downward, however, ask yourself if you have done the exercises with all the necessary rigor and concentration.

In any case, this part of Brain Fitness is not an independent whole: it must be accompanied by exercises in everyday life. Ultimately, cerebral activation must be an integral part of your life.

That will be the subject of the last part of this book: "Brain Fitness in Life."

BRAIN FITNESS
IN LIFE

mproving your mental efficiency so that you can meet the constant challenges of modern life.

Acquiring a sharp, vigorous mind that will enable you to overcome the annoying difficulties of everyday living.

No longer depending on others in family or social life, but taking full responsibility for yourself as an individual.

Preparing yourself to cope with troubles that may come your way.

All those objectives of Brain Fitness cannot be achieved, as I have said, solely by doing the exercises. The exercises are necessary but not sufficient. You must also "live" your Brain Fitness, both by practicing personal activation—which will bring you into indispensable contact with other people—and by adopting a certain philosophy. But this requires that you bring together all the necessary advantages by practicing a specific form of life hygiene.

The final part of this book will therefore be devoted to day-by-day activation and the life hygiene that must accompany it.

DAY-BY-DAY ACTIVATION

Traveling to and from work, doing housework, shopping—all through the day, you can do activation exercises that you devise yourself, depending on circumstances and your imagination.

Combine them, paying special attention to practicing the activities in which you are weakest.

These activities, which involve short-term and long-term memory in varying degrees, will continue the ones you have practiced in the preceding exercises.

PERCEPTIVE ACTIVITY

The goal is to exercise your five senses in such a way as to make them function precisely and rapidly.

Each day, observe an object (a poster, for example) or a person chosen at random. Draw it, him, or her immediately (short-term memory). At the end of the week, re-create your drawings of the seven persons or objects you have chosen (long-term memory).

On the telephone, practice instantly recognizing the people who call you, before they have told you who they are. In the evening, make a list of your successes and failures and use it to memorize the names and phone numbers of the people with whom you have talked. At the end of the week, write down your scores for remembering and forgetting. Later, compare your various scores and graphs showing your progress.

Pay attention to how people you know are dressed; note the shapes and colors of their clothes, and when they change them. Memorize the details in the evening and at the end of the week, and write down your scores.

In your usual restaurant, try to recall the dishes offered (with their prices, if you want to make the exercise harder) without looking at the menu. In the evening, remember as many of them as you can, and write down your score.

When you are out during the day, estimate the number of people you see in different categories (bareheaded or not, for example) and memorize the colors of their clothes, hair, etc. Keep daily and weekly scores.

Practice identifying your neighbors, or the people you work with, by their voices. You will see that rapid progress can be made. In the evening, draw up a list of the men, women, and children you have heard, indicating the characteristics of their voices.

More generally, learn to identify the various sources of sound in your usual surroundings. You will discover that even if you live in the midst of what seems to you a confused, anonymous hubbub, you are capable of quickly discerning specific sounds.

Also exercise your senses of touch (recognizing objects with your eyes closed) and smell.

VISUOSPATIAL ACTIVITY

Its purpose is to develop your ability to make quick and accurate estimates of distances, areas, volumes, and, in general, the proportions of things and their distribution in space.

When you walk into a room where there are a certain number of people, try to determine very quickly how many are on your left and how many are on your right, as well as the left-right distribution of the furniture and other objects.

When you are about to take a picture, before adjusting the focus estimate the distance from the lens to the persons or things you want to photograph, then compare your estimate with the figure given by the camera.

In general, try all through the day to determine how far you are from buildings, cars, people, and so on.

Observe objects—pencils, for example—and try to classify them in relation to their length or thickness.

When you have gone somewhere and come home, take a sheet of paper and try to draw a plan or map of where you were. Do the same exercise the next day, and the day after.

From memory, draw a plan of your workplace, and specifically the room in which you work. You can go further and try to recall everything in your office. Even though those things are familiar to you and form part of your everyday life, you will probably be surprised to discover that you have forgotten many of them, for the great enemy of mental acuity is habit: it dulls our senses.

STRUCTURALIZATION ACTIVITY

To structuralize is to build a logical whole from disparate elements. It is thus an art of synthesis, but it requires close analytic observation of the elements.

Take a sentence in a newspaper: it forms a logical whole. Try to make another sentence with the same words.

Buy a jigsaw puzzle and practice fitting the pieces together as quickly as possible. Or take a sheet of paper on which something is printed or written, cut it into pieces at random, scatter the pieces over a table, and try to reassemble them, guided by their shapes and the meaning of the words.

Practice with one of the many puzzles (a tangram, for example) whose solutions require forming a certain two-dimensional or three-dimensional figure from various components.

You can also take an interest in mathematics, which makes extensive use of structuralization, especially in arithmetic. Mental calculation is therefore advisable. Use it as often as you can when you are shopping—it may have the added advantage of saving you money now and then.

LOGICAL ACTIVITY

Logic is the art of reasoning, the thread of coherence that binds things together. It is rather close to structuralization, with the difference that in logic we are concerned not so much with assembling elements into a whole as with finding an orderly sequence—like Tom Thumb following his trail of pebbles.

Logical activities involve a strategy and lead to social relations. The strategy is the use of a series of coordinated activities to achieve a specific purpose. Take the example of shopping: don't use a list, but if you know you may forget something, invent a system that will take the place of a list. You can use memory aids, such as forming a complete word, or one that can be completed by adding a certain vowel or consonant, from the first letters of the words for the things you need to buy. If you have three things to buy in each store, remember which things come from which store. Or you can classify foods into raw and cooked. And so on. It is up to you to invent memory aids that provide good exercise in mental efficiency.

Games—all games—involve logical activities. I recommend playing them: card games such as pinochle or bridge, chess, checkers, the Japanese game of go, crossword puzzles. The list could go on.

You must be sure to avoid habit, which, as we know, is the great enemy of mental acuity. Although playing is good, always playing the same thing gives rise to routine, which is the opposite of activation. Chess players tend to play only chess, and people who like games based on numbers or letters have the same tendency to stick to their games. In those cases it is always the same cerebral circuits and neuronal regions that function, and everything else sleeps, with the risk of never waking up.

What should you do? Take an interest in activities *that you do not know*. Find new partners for new games. This involves coming out of your shell, going to see what is happening in places outside your little sphere, making contact with others, and weaving new social relations.

VERBAL ACTIVITY

Its purpose is training you to use spoken or written words precisely in referring to concrete realities and abstract concepts. In doing so, it makes extensive demands on short-term and long-term memory.

In the morning, listen carefully to a radio news broadcast. In the course of the day, try to write down the main points of the news that you still remember. Same operation in the evening. Then write down your score.

When you read a newspaper in the morning, memorize things in it, then see how well you remember them when you come home from work.

Whenever you meet someone, try to come up with at least one anagram of his or her name. When you see a word, any word, quickly find others that begin with the same two (or even three) letters.

In any situation of everyday life, try to think of the right terms to describe it: adjectives, nouns, expressions.

Each time you come to the end of a chapter in a book you are reading, imagine that you must summarize it as briefly as possible, orally or in writing, to someone who has not read it. Do the same for the whole book when you have finished it. This is a good exercise not only for verbal activity, but for structuralization and memorization as well. You can also draw up a list of the characters, describing their personalities and the parts they play in the story.

To overcome monotony and routine, which generate lethargy, resignation, and eventually cerebral hypoefficiency, it is not enough to "practice scales." You must also become involved and organize your life in such a way as to open yourself to others through dialogue, interaction, and confrontation. The social is the necessary complement of the individual.

Let us imagine a typical day in the life of a woman in her fifties, a homemaker who wants to remain active and self-sufficient.

In the morning she should not regard getting dressed and grooming herself as a monotonous activity, a kind of drudgery. She should take an interest in her appearance, put on makeup, and try to produce the most attractive image of herself—because it requires an excellent effort of concentration, and also because it is already an opening up to the world, a way of coming out of her shell.

Then she does her shopping. No list, as we know, but an effort to memorize what she needs. No matter if she forgets something and has to go out again—next time, she will most likely think more carefully beforehand and make a better effort to search her memory.

She can develop strategies while she is shopping. For example, she can work out a route that will enable her to avoid doubling back, or crossing a certain dangerous intersection. No monostrategy: she should change her route as often as possible, noting her times of departure and arrival so that she can compare different itineraries.

When she comes home, if she lives alone, she can write down unusual things she has seen; keeping a diary is an excellent idea. If she lives with someone, she can tell in detail about the people and things she has seen.

Now comes the crucial period: the afternoon.

She should avoid passively watching television. She can choose a program that interests her and afterward write a summary of it, or practice describing it to someone, precisely and concisely.

It will be even better for her to go out and take part in the life of the society around her. There are organizations to help her; clubs for older people, for example. Though many are excellent, others are open to criticism because they treat their members like children. And, of course, in such clubs one meets only people of a single generation who all have to cope with the same problems, which means that there is a danger of falling back into monotony. A mixture of ages is much better.

I recommend associations or meeting places where people of different generations (ideally, from childhood to old age) come together to pursue a common interest, such as photography, archaeology, or artistic activities. Under these conditions, age barriers are quickly and easily overcome.

I would urge our hypothetical woman to get a list of the social and cultural organizations in her town or city (she will probably be surprised to learn that they are much more numerous and varied than she thought). Then she can choose one or two, or try out several of them; even if the trials have negative results, they will still be useful experiences.

I would also urge her to try new activities that seem attractive to her, even if she feels she has no ability for them. She must never say, "I can't do it." That sentence should be banished from her speech! With a little effort and persistence, she will soon see that she is quite capable of learning new ways and discovering new worlds.

Coming out of her shell can also involve traveling (there are now all sorts of organized tours at reasonable prices).

If she prefers to be with her friends rather than joining a group, they can plan outings together: exhibitions, films, lectures, etc.

Then comes the night. It is safe to assume that after such a well-filled day she will sleep well and get up the next morning with a cheerful outlook, ready for another day rich in conviviality.

YOUR LIFE HYGIENE

A sprinter may be trained to run a hundred meters in less than ten seconds, but if he is not properly nourished, if he becomes used to drinking a certain amount of alcohol every day, or if he comes to the stadium tired, mentally or physically, he will not perform at the desired level, even if he is the world's most gifted athlete.

Similarly, if you want to carry on your cerebral activity under the best conditions, you must try to give yourself every advantage by supplying your brain with the nutrients it needs: they are its friends.

You must protect it against all the poisons that may disturb its functioning: they are its enemies.

And you must learn to overcome fatigue by increasing your alertness, strengthening memorization and sleeping well.

Before discussing the brain's friends and enemies, which are directly related to the foods we eat, it will be useful to say a few words about dietetics, particularly as it concerns people over the age of fifty.

In the course of aging, the functioning of the stomach and the intestines deteriorates. Gastric acidity, the size of the intestine, assimilation of nutrients, the activity of the digestive juices—all these things are diminished. As a result, the supply of calories is also diminished. Since the aging person's physical and mental activity has not necessarily diminished—or not proportionately, at least—a deficiency is produced. To correct it, people over fifty should, theoretically, eat 20 percent to 25 percent more in order to maintain a good level of physical and mental activity.

This usually does not happen, and sometimes there is a weight loss indicating that the body has begun to use up its reserves, which is not good. Furthermore, an inadequate supply of certain substances may cause disorders. That is the case with phosphorus and calcium: a deficiency of them often causes an excessively high rate of fractures, particularly of the femur.

In addition to all this, there is deterioration of the teeth, which causes insufficient chewing and therefore bad digestion. It also tends to make people overcook their food, so that it will be very tender. Unfortunately, while it is true that green beans cooked for three quarters of an hour are easier to chew, that harsh treatment makes them lose their vitamins. So you should take good care of your teeth, or, if you have dentures, make sure they fit properly.

It also should be noted that the sense of taste changes with time. As we grow older, we have an increased liking for pastry, candy, and sweet drinks. Since eating too much sugar can cause certain disorders, we should try to resist temptation.

Finally, the more people age, the more monotonous their diet becomes. For both practical reasons (difficulties in shopping, money problems) and psychological reasons (fatigue, routine), they fall into the habit of always eating the same foods. A good diet, however, requires a great variety of foods, to make sure we get the substances needed to avoid deficiencies. Because of this, single-food diets (for example, those consisting almost entirely of dairy products or certain fruits) can be harmful. There is no ideal food containing everything we need. Since we are lucky enough to live in a culture that customarily defines a meal as different courses followed by dessert (to which I prefer fruit), we should take advantage of it and be wary of "miracle cures" that may severely damage our bodies. Before plunging into anything of that sort, take the precaution of consulting your doctor.

We can now consider the friends and enemies of good cerebral functioning and neuroplasticity.

For its usual functioning, aside from any exercise of neuronal activation, the brain needs energy, which is supplied primarily by glucose (it also uses oxygen, whose function is to permit metabolism, like the air that serves to burn gasoline in an engine).

Glucose comes from foods rich in sugar. Since there should not be too much of it in the blood, it is better to use slow sugars than fast ones. Slow sugars (supplied by starches, for example) release glucose into the blood at a low rate and provide the brain with stable and continuous energy. Fast sugars (such as sucrose, the refined white sugar sold in stores) pass into the blood rapidly and are quickly metabolized. They give the brain a sudden surge of energy, like high-octane fuel in a racing car. That is why some athletes eat this kind of sugar before a game in which they will have to make rapid, strenuous efforts. They increase the amount of glucose in their blood at the cost of being overwhelmed with fatigue after the game, for the body dislikes that sudden influx.

When the amount of glucose in the blood rises abruptly (hyperglycemia), the body reacts by secreting insulin, which lowers the amount with equal abruptness, and this can easily result in hypoglycemia.

We can see an example of hypoglycemia in everyday life. For breakfast, some people have a cup of heavily sugared coffee without eating anything substantial. Then they go to work. By about eleven o'clock the fast sugar has been metabolized, and the coffee, having stimulated the whole body, including the brain, causes a sudden drop in the blood's glucose level. The effect can be powerful: some people come close to fainting. This phenomenon is well known in hospitals. They have their daily quota of patients in an eleven o'clock daze, who need only to be given a little sugar in order to restore the glucose in their blood to a normal level.

Many people are wise enough to eat a substantial breakfast and make frequent use of slow sugars (such as brown sugar, which, being less refined, contains impurities and is therefore released less rapidly).

Since oxygen is required for metabolizing glucose, we must make sure that we have an adequate supply of it. It interacts with glucose in the blood vessels, but its passage into the blood from inhaled air takes place in the lungs. We must therefore keep our respiratory system in good condition, to ensure that we absorb enough oxygen. The more the lungs are extended and in good condition, the better the transfer of oxygen from the air to the blood takes place.

People who do not get enough exercise diminish their thoracic capacity and therefore the amount of air they breathe. Smokers not only hinder their breathing (tobacco damages the lungs) but may also impair vascularization: blood is inadequately supplied to the brain and the neurons, which consequently may develop lesions.

Cerebral activation increases the brain's need for energy. It must continue to receive its usual nutrients, but in larger quantities, because the risks of deficiencies are greater—it is like going from a subcompact to a racing car.

Calcium is needed to ensure that the neurotransmitters are well synthesized, then released at the synapses.* There also must be precursors, such as choline, which is found in a derivative form in the lecithin of eggs and soybeans.

We also need enzymes, substances that enable the human body to produce the rapid chemical reactions necessary to its function-

---

* I have chosen not to redefine all these terms each time they appear, so that you can train your memory. If it fails you, turn back to the chapter on the cerebral mechanism, but try not to do it too often.

ing. To produce those same reactions without enzymes, the body would have to increase its temperature from 98.6°F to more than 400°! Enzymes are in everyone's body, but to be effective they need coenzymes, among which are certain substances—zinc, copper, selenium, cobalt—known as trace elements. We need only minute amounts of them. They are found in dried fruits, dried or fresh vegetables, etc.

Again we see the advantage of having a varied diet, eating a little of everything, to enrich the body's stock of necessary substances and to avoid deficiencies.

But the synapses also have enemies. Whereas calcium favors the release of neurotransmitters, as we have seen, aluminum and the heavy metals block the system. They are found in some tap water and in certain medicines. Bismuth, which was once used to treat gastric disorders, sometimes caused brain diseases. People who still use it regularly should be warned against its harmful effects in large doses.

Tobacco is also an enemy, not only of the synapses but also of cerebral functioning in general. First of all, nicotine in high doses blocks the action of the neurotransmitters, much as aluminum does. It also blocks brain receptors, which results in lesions and degeneration. Finally, tar damages the lungs and therefore indirectly diminishes the amount of oxygen that the brain receives.

In very small amounts, alcohol stimulates the functioning of the synapses. In larger amounts it has an opposite effect: the synapses slow their exchanges and lapse into a kind of quiescence. It creates habituation and therefore dependency: the more one drinks, the larger the amount of alcohol one needs to reach the threshold of excitation.

The neuronal membranes must also be vitalized and reinvigorated by an increased supply of ions. Two ions are indispensable: those of calcium and magnesium. Calcium and magnesium are found in dairy products. Magnesium is also found in dried fruits, grapes, etc.

The neuronal membranes also need lipids and protides. Lipids, or, more specifically, phospholipids, are found in dairy products (especially sheep's milk cheese), meat, and fish. The amino acid content of these phospholipids, and of the triglycerides, varies with the origins of our foods.

For reconstruction of the brain's elements, and to ensure that it takes place under good conditions, different fatty acids are required. This means that we should use different cooking and salad oils (peanut, sunflower, olive, etc.). Each of them gives us a specific constructive element. People who always consume the same kind of oil not only risk falling into routine, but they give their neuronal membranes only one type of fatty acid, which may lead to a deficiency. It is known, for example, that when rats are given only one kind of oil, their learning ability decreases.

As for protides, they are found in meat—but here, too, different kinds should be eaten (beef, mutton, pork, poultry). The more we age, the more protides we need; and so, contrary to what one might think, older people should increase their meat consumption. Vegetarians can, of course, replace meat with eggs, which are only a stage in the development of meat. They also can choose to eat "steak" made of soybeans or alfalfa. That is what cattle do: they absorb amino acids from those plant foods and turn them into meat. But it is not certain that the taste of such meat substitutes will give as much pleasure as that of meat itself, and, without pleasure, eating is only a chore.

The enemies of reinvigoration of the neuronal membranes are toxic, unstable molecules called free radicals. The enemies of these enemies are certain vitamins. They are worth dwelling on awhile.

We live in a world where more and more processed foods are consumed. They are not inherently bad, and I prefer canned green beans to green beans that have been on display in a store for several days, but fresh foods are best because they contain more vitamins. Remember one thing, however: if they are overcooked, or kept hot too long, their vitamins are destroyed.

We should become used to eating raw vegetables: tomatoes, cabbage, carrots, etc. Or we should at least cook them as little as possible (hence the value of nouvelle cuisine, which often prepares them al dente and lets us discover their real taste).* Vegetables that have been quick-frozen and properly preserved also contain vitamins—not as many as fresh vegetables, but more than canned ones.

Let us now consider the main vitamins that are useful to the brain system.

Vitamin B_6 helps all cells to utilize amino acids and plays an important part in sleep. It is found in liver, kidneys, brains, grains, bananas, and green vegetables.

Vitamin B_{12}, found in liver (poultry liver, for example), fish, and meat, should be taken at the same time as vitamin B_6. It is involved in the making of red corpuscles.

Vitamin C, the vitamin of alertness, helps the body to defend itself against fatigue and various bacteria. It is found in citrus fruits, lettuce, and liver. A small amount is sufficient.**

Vitamin E eliminates the free radicals that are enemies of the neuronal membranes. This "youth vitamin" is found in cooking oil, butter, and all other dairy products, green vegetables, and the germs of grains.

Besides vitamins, a number of other substances are useful to cerebral activation. I will mention the main ones.

First, sodium chloride, commonly known simply as salt. It is one of the substances that older people most often lack. Contrary to what is said here and there, salt consumed in moderate amounts has never harmed anyone. While certain medicines require following a diet (and the doctor is there to advise and prescribe), people sometimes take it upon themselves to give up salt without telling their doctor about it. Actually, it is safe to consume salt if you drink enough liquids, which enables the body to eliminate

---

* Rapid cooking in a microwave oven is certainly preferable to slow cooking.
** Caution: Too much Vitamin C can cause nervousness and anxiety.

any excess. In any case, a saltless diet causes weight reduction by loss of water—which can also be obtained by drinking more water.

Other substances useful to cerebral activation:

Salts of calcium (phosphates, sulfates), which are needed for the proper formation of bone and are found in dairy products. Salts of iron (in watercress, carrots, spinach, onions, leeks, cabbage, asparagus, chicory), fluorine (in asparagus, barley, tomatoes, potatoes, Roquefort cheese), and phosphorus (in garlic, barley, cabbage, spinach, onions, lettuce, carrots, potatoes, strawberries, raspberries, tomatoes, artichokes).

Providing your brain with the substances required for its nourishment and the extra effort of activation is not enough for your life hygiene. You must also be able to overcome fatigue, which can impair cerebral functioning and make neuronal activation futile.

To do that, the first step is to increase your alertness. If you have all your wits about you from the time you get up in the morning, you will be able to adjust to any situation. If you drink coffee at breakfast, add slow-acting sugar to it or eat fruit with it. A breakfast consisting entirely of unsweetened coffee or tea is a dietary aberration. You should fill your stomach, because it must hold out till lunch.

Some substances are reputed to increase alertness. Thyme is one (Charlemagne consumed a great deal of it) and so is rosemary (of which Madame de Sévigné said, "I am mad about it"). Vitamin C is also a cerebral stimulant; lemon juice taken several times a day is good for the brain.

You should also know that some substances can strengthen memory. Fish, for example, is traditionally recommended for that purpose (probably because of the beneficial effect of phosphorus on neurons). There are "memory herb teas" made with mint, basil, or wild thyme. These plants can also be taken in the form of spices.

Finally, to have an effective memory and produce cerebral

activation, we must be in good physical condition. If we are tired, neurotransmitters are released at a lower rate and there is a general slowing of activity. So it is important to avoid overexertion and get plenty of good sleep.

Do not try to get it artificially, though, with sleeping pills. They should be used only in exceptional circumstances. When they are overused, they cause sluggish awakening in the morning and drowsiness all through the day, which can be dangerous (if you must drive a car, for example). Once you have formed the habit of taking them every night, you soon find that you must increase the dose, and this gradually increases your dependence on them.

To get a good night's sleep, you must have had a good day in which you were active and involved. It is better not to take a nap, unless you deduct it from your hours of sleep at night.

Since you normally sleep better on an empty stomach, you should have your evening meal at least an hour before you go to bed. You can also drink a lightly sedative herb tea. Avoid coffee and other stimulants.

We have now come to the end of this book. I have tried to make it clear and simple, but also well documented and accurate—and optimistic: your health and the success of your life are now in your hands.

Use this book as a tool, a means of bettering your performance.

Maybe it will become a faithful friend and a witness to your success.

That is what I hope for it.

That is what I hope for you with all my heart.

ACKNOWLEDGMENTS

I would like to thank, for their patient collaboration, all my col-leagues in the INRPVC, and particularly the "veterans": Ioannis Lamproglou, Florence Moulin, and Pierre Migeon.

For their critical reading and critical spirit, I would also like to thank Dr. Jean Sotton; Professor Jean-Robert Rapin, phar-macologist; and Professor Christian Derouesne, neurologist at La Pitié-Salpêtrière.

SELECTED READINGS

BOOKS

Boismare, F., Le Poncin, M., Rapin, J.R. "Blockade of the different enzymatic steps in the synthesis of brain amines and learning (CAR) in hypobaric hypoxic. L. Dopa treated rats." *Catecholamine Basic and Clinical Frontiers,* t. II. Usdin, Kopin, Barchas, eds. Pergamon Press, 1979, pp. 1726–1728.

* **Le Poncin-Lafitte, M.** "Visualization de l'hypofonctionnement cérébral et sa récuperation par l'application d'une méthode informatisée d'activation cérébrale (Gym Cerveau)." *Entraînement de la mémoire.* Zurich: Gottlieb Duttweiler Institute, 1987.

* **Le Poncin-Lafitte, M., Aymonod, M., Billon, C., Pesquies, P.C., Rapin, J.R.** "Plasma catecholamine and brain activities." *Catecholamine and Stress: Recent Advances,* Usdin, Kvetnansky, Kopin, eds. Elsevier North Holland Inc., 1980, pp. 227–30.

Le Poncin-Lafitte, M., Boismare, F., Pesquies, P.C., Rapin J.R. "Hypobaric stress and cerebral blood flow (CBF), brain and peripheral catecholamines in rats." *Catecholamine Basic and Clinical Frontiers,* t. I. Usdin, Kopin, Barchas, eds. 1979, pp. 939–41.

Le Poncin-Lafitte, M., Grosdemouge, C., Loison, B., Barreteau, H., Rapin, J.R. "Evidence of the dopaminergic system in microcirculation. Study in vivo." *Cerebral Blood Flow Effects of Nerves and Neurotransmitters,* D.D. Heistad, M.L. Marcus, eds. New York: Elsevier Science Publishing Co., Inc., 1982, pp. 143–51.

---

* Of special interest.

Le Poncin-Lafitte, M., Pesquies, P.C., Billion, C. et Rapin, J.R. "Effects of the blocking of dopaminergic receptors on the cerebral blood flow, the uptake of deoxyglucose and memorization." *Circulation cérébral.* A. Bes, G. Geraud, eds. 1979, pp. 67–69.

* Le Poncin-Lafitte, M., Rancurel, G., Raynaud, C., Migeon, P., Rapin, J.R. "Variability of cerebral blood defects in Alzheimer's disease SPECT studies at rest and during memorization." *Aging: The Universal Human Experience.* Highlights of the 1985 International Congress of Gerontology. New York: Springer Publishing Company, 1987.

Lerner-Natoli, M., Le Poncin-Lafitte, M., Rondouin, G., Rapin, J.R., and Baldy-Moulinier, M. "Simultaneous determinations of local cerebral blood flow and metabolism in the different stages of amygdaloid kindling." *Current Pbs in Epilepsy: I. Cerebral Blood Flow and Metabolism and Epilepsy.* M. Baldy-Moulinier, D.H. Ingvar, B.S. Meldrum, eds. London: John Libby, 1983, pp. 105–11.

Rapin, J.R., Grosdemouge, C., Le Poncin-Lafitte, M. "Distribution of the blood flow in brain areas after a quantitative ischemia in rats." *Pathophysiology and Pharmacotherapy of Cerebrovascular Disorders.* Betz, Grote, Heuser, Wullenweber, eds. Cologne: Verlag Gerhard Witestrock, 1980, pp. 163–66.

Rapin, J.R., Duterte, D., Le Poncin-Lafitte, M. "Modèles d'étude des désordres cérébrovasculaires à l'aide de déoxyglucose 3H," *Radioaktive Isotope in Klinik und Forschung,* t. XIV, Egermann Ed. Verlag, 1980, pp. 269–76.

Vollant, M., Le Poncin-Lafitte, M., Rapin, J.R. "Some specific errors in VRT of Benton in detection of senile dementia of Alzheimer type," *Senile Dementias: Early Detection.* A. Bes, et al., eds. London: John Libby, 1986, pp. 631–35.

JOURNALS

Boismare, F., Le Poncin, M., Belliard, J.P., Hacpille, L. "Reduction of hypoxia induced disturbances by previous treatment with benserazide et L Dopa." *Experientia,* 31 (10), 1975, pp. 1190–92.

Boismare, F., Le Poncin, M., Hacpille, L. "Cardiovascular responses to acute hypoxia in dogs pretreated with benserazide and L Dopa." *Eur. J. Parmacol.,* 38, 1976, pp. 1–5.

Boismare, F., Le Poncin, M., Lefrançois, J., Marchand, J.C. "Bio-

---

* Of special interest.

chemical and behavioral disturbances induced by hypoxia in rats." *Acta Neurol. Scand.,* 56, 1977, suppl. 64.

Boismare, F., Le Poncin, M., Lefrançois, J. "Mémorisation et catéch-olamines centrales après un traumatisme crânio-cervical expérimental chez le rat: influence d'une administration d'imipramine." *Psychopharmacology,* 55, 1977, pp. 251–56.

Boismare, F., Le Poncin, M., Lefrançois, J. "Biochemical and behavioral effects of hypoxia in rats: study of the protection afforded by Ergotalkaloïds." *Gerontology,* 24, suppl. 1, 1978, pp. 6–13.

Boismare, F., Le Poncin, M., Lefrançois, J., Lecordier, J.C. "The action of Cytidine-Diphosphocholine on the functional and hemodynamic effects of cerebral ischemia in rats." *Pharmacology,* 17 (1), 1978, pp. 15–20.

* Derouesne, C., Rancure, G., Le Poncin-Lafitte, M., Rapin, J.R., Lassen, N.A. "Variability of cerebral blood flow defects in Alzheimer's disease on Ido-isopropyl-amphetamine and single photon emission tomography." *The Lancet,* 8440, 1985, p. 1292.

* Hossman, K.A., Mies, G., Pashen, W., Csiba, L., Bodsch, W., Rapin, J.R., Le Poncin-Lafitte, M., Takahashi, K. "Multiparametric imaging of blood flow and metabolism after middle cerebral artery occlusion in rats." *J. Cerebral Blood Flow and Metabolism,* 5, 1985, pp. 97–107.

* Lageron, A., Le Poncin-Lafitte, M., Rapin, J.R. "Brain rat histoenzymological changes induced by microspheres injection during ischemia." *Acta Histochem.,* 65, 1979, pp. 184–90.

Lassen, N.A., Henriksen, L., Holm, S., Barry, D.I., Paulson, O.B., Vorstrup, S., Rapin, J.R., Le Poncin-Lafitte, M., Moretti, J.L. "Central blood flow tomography Xenon 133 compared to Isopropyl-Amphetamine-Iodine-123." *J. Nucl. Med.,* 24 (1), 1983, pp. 17–21.

Le Poncin-Lafitte, M., Boismare, F., Rapin, J.R. "Effects of strangulation on deoxyglucose uptake and blood flow in the rat brain areas." *Acta Neurol. Scand.,* 60, 1979, suppl. 72, pp. 334–35.

Le Poncin, M., Charpentier, J. "Effet de la fumée de tabac par voie respiratoire sur le conditionnement d'évitement chez le rat." *J. Physiologie,* 65, no 3, 1972, 444 A.

Le Poncin-Lafitte, M., Duterte, D., Galiez, V., Lamproglou, Y., Rapin, J.R. "Apprentissage et concomitances hémodynamiques et métaboliques chez l'animal âgé après un accident ischémique aigu." *Presse Méd.,* 12, 1983, pp. 3061–65.

---

* Of special interest.

Le Poncin-Lafitte, M., Grosdemouge, C., Roy-Billon, C., Duterte, D., Potrat, P., Lespinasse, P., Rapin, J.R. "Short term memory and cerebral ischemia: pharmacological application." *Ibid.,* pp. 265–69.

Le Poncin-Lafitte, M., Grosdemouge, C., Roy-Billon, C., Duterte, D., Rapin, J.R. "Hemodynamic, metabolic and functional changes induced by experimental cerebral microinfarction: basic and therapeutic approach." *J. Cerebral Blood Flow and Metabolism,* 1, suppl. 1, 1981, pp. 260–61.

Le Poncin-Lafitte, M., Grosdemouge, C., Duterte, D., Rapin, J.R.: "Simultaneous study of haemodynamic, metabolic and behavioural sequelae in a model of cerebral ischaemia in aged rats: Effects of nicergoline." *Gerontology,* 30, 1984, pp. 109–19.

* Le Poncin-Lafitte, M., Lewrdier, J.C., Rapin, J.R. "Sound avoidance conditioning and a mathematical approach to the description of acquisition performance." *Math. Biosciences,* 59, 1982, pp. 249–68.

Le Poncin-Lafitte, M., Pesquies, P.C. and Rapin, J.R. "Correlation between brain blood flow and catecholamine levels in rat brain areas under hypobaric hypoxia." *Experientia,* 36, 1980, pp. 1405–6.

* Le Poncin-Lafitte, M., Rapin, J.R. "Age and Learning: Experimental and clinical aspects." *Gerontology,* 32, suppl. 1, 1986, pp. 53–59.

Le Poncin-Lafitte, M., Rapin, J.R. "Age associated changes in deoxyglucose uptake in whole brain." *Gerontology,* 26, 1980, pp. 265–69.

* Le Poncin-Lafitte, M., Raynaud, C., Derouesne, C., Rancurel, G., Rapin, J.R. "Variability of cerebral blood flow defects in Alzheimer's disease seen by 123 Iodo-isopropyl-amphetamine and SPECT: studies at rest and during memorization." *J. Cerebral Blood Flow and Metabolism,* 5, suppl. 1, 1985, pp. 135–36.

Lespinasse, P., Le Poncin-Lafitte, M., Pesquies, P.C. and Rapin, J.R. "Demonstration of vascular redistribution after carotid clamping in rats." *Experientia,* 39, 1983, pp. 369–371.

Nicolaidis, S., Le Poncin-Lafitte, M., Danguir, J., Grosdemouge, C., Rapin, J.R. "Specific behaviors bound brain cartography of the glucose uptake in rats." *Ibid.,* pp. 180–82.

Rapin, J.R., Duterte, D., Le Poncin-Lafitte, M., Lageron, A., Monmaur, P., Rips, R., Lassen, N.A. "Iodoamphetamine derivatives as tracers for local cerebral blood flow or not? Autoradiographic and autohistoradiographic studies." *J. Cerebral Blood Flow and Metabolism,* 3, suppl. 1, 1983, pp. 105–6.

* Of special interest.

Rapin, J.R., Lageron, A., Le Poncin-Lafitte, M. "Deoxyglucose uptake in pathological conditions." *European Neurology,* 20, 1981, pp. 146–51.

Rapin, J.R., Le Poncin-Lafitte, M., Duterte, D., Rips, R., Morier, E., Lassen, N.A. "Iodoamphetamine as a new tracer for local cerebral blood flow in the rat: Comparison with Isopropyliodoamphetamine." *J. Cerebral Blood Flow and Metabolism,* 4, 1984, pp. 270–74.

* Rapin, J.R., Le Poncin-Lafitte, M., Lespinasse, P. "Simultaneous study of cerebral blood flow, vascular and deoxyglucose in aged rats." *Pharmacology,* 28, 1984, pp. 241–50.

Rapin, J.R., Le Poncin-Lafitte, M., Pesquies, P.C. "Cerebral blood flow redistribution in rats during hypobaric hypoxia." *Acta Neurol. Scand.,* 60, 1979, suppl. 72, pp. 322–23.

PAPERS

Le Poncin-Lafitte, M. "Imaging of functional brain in aging—clinical and experimental aspects (abstract)," I P A Congress (congrès de psychogériatrie), Chicago, 27–31 Aug. 1987.

---

* Of special interest.